# SAP® Crystal Reports® 2016: Part 2

# SAP® Crystal Reports® 2016: Part 2

Part Number: 095203
Course Edition: 1.0

## Acknowledgements

### PROJECT TEAM

| Author | Media Designer | Content Editor |
| --- | --- | --- |
| Michelle Wescott | Brian J. Sullivan | Joe McElveney |

## Notices

# SAP® Crystal Reports® 2016: Part 2

# About This Course

Until now, you have used Crystal Reports to build and modify reports. You want to use the advanced functionality of Crystal Reports to generate reports in the format you desire. In this course, you will create complex reports and data sources using the tools in Crystal Reports 2016. You will not only create more sophisticated reports including subreports and cross-tabs, but you will also increase the speed and efficiency of your reports by using SQL queries.

Even though you are familiar with Crystal Reports, you may take some time to study its various tools that enable you to generate reports with the desired data using advanced methods such as SQL querying. This way, you won't be slowed down by large databases or databases with which you are unfamiliar. By creating subreports, cross-tabs, and running totals, you will turn raw data into meaningful customized reports that will help your business run more smoothly. If you work with large databases, you may find yourself faced with performance issues. In this course, you will also learn to use tools that can increase the speed with which data is retrieved.

## Course Description

### Target Student

This course is designed for people who know how to create basic list and group reports and need to create reports that include subreports, cross-tabs, advanced formulas, and charts based on more than one data series. They may also need to build tools that make it easier for other people to create reports. They may or may not have programming and/or SQL experience.

### Course Prerequisites

To ensure your success, a knowledge of programming and/or SQL would also be helpful. You can also take the following Logical Operations course:

- *SAP® Crystal Reports® 2016: Part 1*

### Course Objectives

In this course, you will create complex reports using tools in Crystal Reports 2016.

You will:

- Create automatic and manual running totals.
- Work with cross-tab reports.
- Add subreports.
- Create drill-downs in a report.
- Use SQL statements in report processing.

- Create complex formulas.
- Add charts to reports.
- Enhance report functionality.

# The CHOICE Home Screen

Logon and access information for your CHOICE environment will be provided with your class experience. The CHOICE platform is your entry point to the CHOICE learning experience, of which this course manual is only one part.

On the CHOICE Home screen, you can access the CHOICE Course screens for your specific courses. Visit the CHOICE Course screen both during and after class to make use of the world of support and instructional resources that make up the CHOICE experience.

Each CHOICE Course screen will give you access to the following resources:

- **Classroom**: A link to your training provider's classroom environment.
- **eBook**: An interactive electronic version of the printed book for your course.
- **Files**: Any course files available to download.
- **Checklists**: Step-by-step procedures and general guidelines you can use as a reference during and after class.
- **Spotlights**: Brief animated videos that enhance and extend the classroom learning experience.
- **Assessment**: A course assessment for your self-assessment of the course content.
- Social media resources that enable you to collaborate with others in the learning community using professional communications sites such as LinkedIn or microblogging tools such as Twitter.

Depending on the nature of your course and the components chosen by your learning provider, the CHOICE Course screen may also include access to elements such as:

- LogicalLABS, a virtual technical environment for your course.
- Various partner resources related to the courseware.
- Related certifications or credentials.
- A link to your training provider's website.
- Notices from the CHOICE administrator.
- Newsletters and other communications from your learning provider.
- Mentoring services.

Visit your CHOICE Home screen often to connect, communicate, and extend your learning experience!

# How to Use This Book

### As You Learn

This book is divided into lessons and topics, covering a subject or a set of related subjects. In most cases, lessons are arranged in order of increasing proficiency.

The results-oriented topics include relevant and supporting information you need to master the content. Each topic has various types of activities designed to enable you to solidify your understanding of the informational material presented in the course. Information is provided for reference and reflection to facilitate understanding and practice.

Data files for various activities as well as other supporting files for the course are available by download from the CHOICE Course screen. In addition to sample data for the course exercises, the course files may contain media components to enhance your learning and additional reference materials for use both during and after the course.

Checklists of procedures and guidelines can be used during class and as after-class references when you're back on the job and need to refresh your understanding.

At the back of the book, you will find a glossary of the definitions of the terms and concepts used throughout the course. You will also find an index to assist in locating information within the instructional components of the book.

## As You Review

Any method of instruction is only as effective as the time and effort you, the student, are willing to invest in it. In addition, some of the information that you learn in class may not be important to you immediately, but it may become important later. For this reason, we encourage you to spend some time reviewing the content of the course after your time in the classroom.

## As a Reference

The organization and layout of this book make it an easy-to-use resource for future reference. Taking advantage of the glossary, index, and table of contents, you can use this book as a first source of definitions, background information, and summaries.

## Course Icons

Watch throughout the material for the following visual cues.

| Icon | Description |
| --- | --- |
| | A **Note** provides additional information, guidance, or hints about a topic or task. |
| | A **Caution** note makes you aware of places where you need to be particularly careful with your actions, settings, or decisions so that you can be sure to get the desired results of an activity or task. |
| | **Spotlight** notes show you where an associated Spotlight is particularly relevant to the content. Access Spotlights from your CHOICE Course screen. |
| | **Checklists** provide job aids you can use after class as a reference to perform skills back on the job. Access checklists from your CHOICE Course screen. |
| | **Social** notes remind you to check your CHOICE Course screen for opportunities to interact with the CHOICE community using social media. |

# 1 | Creating Running Totals

**Lesson Time: 1 hour, 50 minutes**

## Lesson Objectives

In this lesson, you will:

- Create a running total field.
- Modify a running total field.
- Create a manual running total.

## Lesson Introduction

You presented totals as summary information appearing at the bottom of a report and in a group section. Another way to create specialized summaries is to use running totals.

You may want to calculate the volume of sales in your report. By creating running totals, you will be able to track data incrementally.

# TOPIC A

## Create a Running Total Field

You used functions and arrays to retrieve data from reports. You may now want to calculate the total for a particular field in the retrieved data.

Calculating the totals of all the records in a group manually is a time-consuming process. Creating a running total field will enable you to get the totals within a short span of time.

### Running Totals

A *running total* is a summary value that is displayed for each record. It totals the values for a selected field in a report or group, up to and including the current record. A running total name can contain mixed characters and spaces.

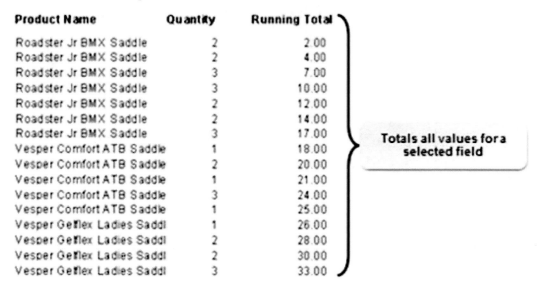

Figure 1–1: A running total field displayed in a report.

### The Create Running Total Field Dialog Box

The **Create Running Total Field** dialog box has components, such as sections and text boxes, that you can use to enter required information to create a running total.

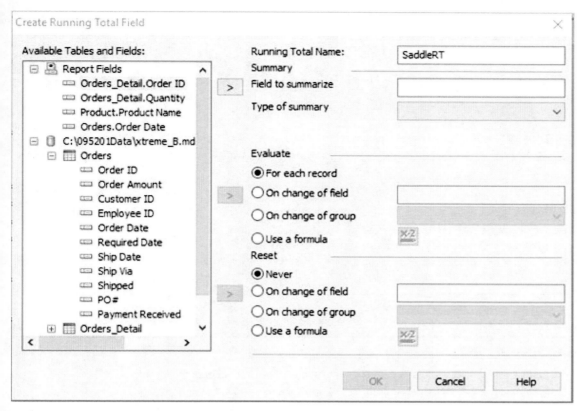

*Figure 1-2: The Create Running Total Field dialog box.*

| Component | Allows You To |
| --- | --- |
| The **Running Total Name** text box | Provide a name to the running total. |
| The **Field to summarize** text box | Select the desired field whose data is to be summarized. |
| The **Type of summary** drop-down list | Determine the type of summary operation to be performed on the selected field. |
| The **Evaluate** section | Determine when the running total should be increased. The default setting is to increment the running total on each record. You can use the other options to calculate the increment whenever a field or a group in a report is modified. You can also increment running totals based on a formula that you have created. For example, increase the incremental running total only when the customer region field is equal to CA. |
| The **Reset** section | Determine the time when a running total field should be reset to zero. The default setting is not to perform a reset. You can use the other options to reset the running total whenever a field or a group in a report is modified. You can also reset the running total based on a formula. For example, in a report showing cumulative sales for the last two years, reset the sales total to zero at the beginning of each year. |

> **Access the Checklist tile on your CHOICE Course screen for reference information and job aids on How to Create a Running Total Field.**

# ACTIVITY 1–1
## Creating a Running Total Field

### Data Files

C:\095203Data\Creating Running Totals\RT Saddle Sales.rpt

C:\095203Data\xtreme_B.mdb

### Scenario

You work for a company that sells bicycles and related equipment, and you are in charge of the inventory for bicycle saddles. Orders are piling up, and you need to set up a delivery schedule with your supplier. To make sure you are not overstocked or short, you want to calculate the cumulative total of the saddle quantities sold, along with the details of items, in order to view order trends.

> **Note:** Activities may vary slightly if the software vendor has issued digital updates. Your instructor will notify you of any changes.

1. Create a formula for calculating the cumulative total of the saddle quantities sold.
   a) Launch the SAP® Crystal Reports® 2016 application.
   b) Maximize the window.
   c) Display the **Open** dialog box.
   d) Navigate to the **C:\095203Data\Creating Running Totals** folder.
   e) Select the **RT Saddle Sales.rpt** file, and then select **Open**.

   f) In the **Field Explorer**, select **Running Total Fields**, and then select the **New** button.
   g) In the **Create Running Total Field** dialog box, in the **Running Total Name** text box, type *SaddleRT*
   h) In the **Available Tables and Fields** list box, select **Orders_Detail.Quantity**, and then select the first right-arrow button to add the selected field to the **Field to summarize** text box.
   i) In the **Type of summary** drop-down list, verify that **sum** is displayed.
   j) In the **Evaluate** section, verify that the **For each record** option is selected.
   k) In the **Reset** section, verify that the **Never** option is selected.
   l) Select **OK** to create the running total field.

2. Place the formula in the **Details** section and label it *Running Total*.
   a) Select the **Design** tab, and from the **Field Explorer**, select and drag the **SaddleRT** running total field approximately to the 4.5-inch mark in the **Details** section.
   b) Select and drag the middle-right sizing handle of the **SaddleRT** field to the 6-inch mark.
   c) Double-click the **SaddleRT** field heading.
   d) Select the existing text and type *Running Total*
   e) Click anywhere in the report area to deselect the field.

3. Format the items in the page header.
   a) In the **Page Header (PH)** section, select the **Quantity** text object.

   b) On the **Standard** toolbar, select the **Format Painter** button.
   c) Select the **Running Total** field heading to apply the formatting.
   d) Verify that the **Running Total** field heading looks similar to the **Quantity** text object.
   e) In the blue area of the **PH** section, right-click and select the **Select All Section Objects** option.
   f) Select **Format→Align→Tops** to align all the text objects.

g) Preview the report.

h) In the running total field, select the first record, and on the **Formatting** toolbar, select the **Decrease Decimals** button twice.

i) Save the report as *My RT Saddle Sales*

# TOPIC B

## Modify a Running Total Field

You inserted a running total field in your report. The running total doesn't provide the desired results, so you decide to alter the running total field to suit your requirements.

The Sales report contains a running total that calculates a sum of the total sales made during that year. However, management wants you to calculate the average sales made during a particular time period. In this case, you just need to modify the existing running total field.

 **Access the Checklist tile on your CHOICE Course screen for reference information and job aids on How to Modify a Running Total Field.**

# ACTIVITY 1-2
## Modifying a Running Total Field

### Data File
C:\095203Data\xtreme_B.mdb

### Before You Begin
The My RT Saddle Sales.rpt file is open.

### Scenario
You have a report that contains sales data for a three-year period. You need to display the sales data in your report for each quarter to prepare a detailed report. You also want to find out the total sales on Saturdays because it's your peak business day. Because there are no Saturdays until the fifth record, the related fields appear blank for that sale. You decide to hide the sales total when the sale date is not a Saturday.

---

1. Group the report data by calendar quarter.
   a) In the **Design** view, select **Insert→Group**.
   b) In the **Insert Group** dialog box, from the first drop-down list, select **Orders.Order Date**.
   c) In the second drop-down list, verify that **in ascending order** is selected.
   d) In the **The section will be printed** section, from the drop-down list, select **for each quarter**, and then select **OK**.

2. Modify the running total field so that it sums only Saturday sales.
   a) On the **Preview** tab, verify that the running total displays the cumulative total of sales for all days.
   b) Select the **Design** tab.
   c) Right-click the **#SaddleRT** field and select **Edit Running Total**.
   d) In the **Edit Running Total Field** dialog box, in the **Evaluate** section, select the **Use a formula** option, and then select the **Conditional Formula** button. [x·2]
   e) In the **Formula Workshop - Running Total Condition Formula** window, in the **Function Tree**, expand **Functions** and then expand **Date and Time**.
   f) Scroll down, expand **DayOfWeek**, and then double-click **DayOfWeek (date)**.
   g) In the **Field Tree**, under **Report Fields**, expand **C:\095203Data\xtreme_B.mdb (Access/Excel (DAO))**.
   h) Expand **Orders**, and then double-click **Order Date**.
   i) After the last closing parenthesis of the formula, type **=7**
   j) Compare your formula with the following:

      ```
      DayOfWeek ({Orders.Order Date})=7
      ```

   k) Select the **Check** button [x·2] to validate the formula, and in the **SAP Crystal Reports** message box, select **OK**.
   l) Select **Save and close**.
   m) In the **Edit Running Total Field** dialog box, select **OK**.
   n) In the **Confirm Command** message box, select **Yes** to proceed with the changes.
   o) Double-click the **Running Total** field heading, select the text, and type *Saturday Sales*
   p) Click anywhere in the report area to deselect the field heading.
   q) Select the **Preview** tab.
   r) Verify that there is a cumulative increase in sales when a sale is made on a Saturday.

---

3. Suppress the running total field when it's not a Saturday.

   a) Right-click the first running total value and select **Format Field**.

   b) In the **Format Editor** dialog box, select the **Common** tab.

   c) To the right of the **Suppress** check box, select the **Conditional Formula** button.

   d) In the **Formula Workshop - Format Formula Editor - Suppress** window, in the **Function Tree**, double-click **DayOfWeek (date)** to create a formula using the function.

   e) In the **Field Tree**, under **Report Fields**, verify that the **Orders** table is expanded.

   f) Double-click **Order Date** to add the field to the formula.

   g) Click after the last closing parentheses and type **<>7**

   h) Compare your formula with the following:

   ```
   DayOfWeek ({Orders.Order Date})<>7
   ```

   i) Check the formula for errors, and in the **SAP Crystal Reports** message box, select **OK**.

   j) Select **Save and close**.

   k) In the **Format Editor** dialog box, select **OK**.

   l) Verify that the cumulative total of the sales appears only when the order date is a Saturday.

   m) Save the report and switch to the **Design** view.

# ACTIVITY 1–3
## Resetting a Running Total

### Data File
C:\095203Data\xtreme_B.mdb

### Before You Begin
The My RT Saddle Sales.rpt file is open.

### Scenario
The report you created counts all Saturday sales for the entire period of the report. You decide to calculate the Saturday sales within each calendar quarter starting over with a zero at the start of each calendar quarter to help determine staffing needs on Saturdays. You also want to display the running total for each quarter in the report to enhance its readability.

---

1. Modify the running total field so that it resets on each calendar quarter.
   a) In the **Design** view, right-click the **#SaddleRT** field and select **Edit Running Total**.
   b) In the **Edit Running Total Field** dialog box, in the **Reset** section, select the **On change of group** option to reset the running total when the selected group is modified, and then select **OK**.
   c) In the **Confirm Command** message box, select **Yes** to perform the command.
   d) Preview the report.
   e) Verify that the first Saturday in each calendar quarter contains the total for just that sale and the running total is then increased to the next calendar quarter.

2. Display the suppressed running total field in the group footer.
   a) Switch to the **Design** view.
   b) In the **Design** view, right-click the **#SaddleRT** running total field and select **Copy**.
   c) In the **Group Footer #1 (GF1)** section, below the **#SaddleRT** running total field, right-click and select **Paste**, and then click at the 4.5-inch mark to place the running total field.
   d) Preview the report.
   e) Verify that the group footer section displays the cumulative total for only the first group because the running total that you copied is suppressed.

3. Display the cumulative total of the sales quantity for each quarter in the group footer.
   a) Select the **Design** tab.
   b) In the GF1 section, right-click the **#SaddleRT** field and select **Format Field**.
   c) Select the **Common** tab, and to the right of the **Suppress** check box, select the **Conditional Formula** button.
   d) In the **Formula Workshop - Format Formula Editor - Suppress** window, select the formula and delete it.
   e) Select **Save and close**.
   f) In the **Format Editor** dialog box, select **OK**.
   g) Preview the report.
   h) Verify that the report displays the cumulative total of the sales quantity for each quarter in the group footer section and the cumulative total for the Saturday sales in the **Details** section.
   i) Save and close the file.

---

# TOPIC C

## Create a Manual Running Total

You modified a running total to produce the desired results. However, when creating running totals in complex reports, the values may not always be accurate.

Running totals in complex reports containing many group levels or suppressed sections sometimes produce incorrect results. Creating a manual running total ensures that your complex reports are producing accurate data.

### Variables

A *variable* is a storage location in memory whose value can change as an application is running. Before you can use a variable in a formula, you must declare the variable by giving it a type and name. All variable types in the Crystal syntax must end with the var keyword in either lowercase or uppercase. The assignment operator assigns values to variables.

 **Note:** A variable cannot have the same name as any function, operator, or other keyword that is valid in the Crystal syntax. For example, a variable cannot be named *Exp*, because *Exp* is a built-in function.

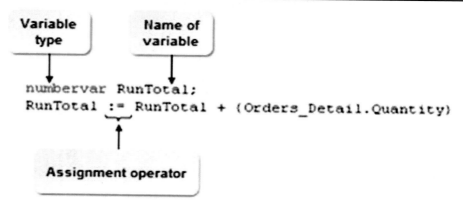

*Figure 1-3: Variables.*

### Variable Syntax

The Crystal syntax used to declare a variable is:

```
typevar variable name;
variable name := value;
```

You can also declare a variable and assign a value to it in one single expression using the following syntax:

```
typevar variable name := value;
```

### Variable Declaration Types

A list of the common variable declaration types used in Crystal Reports formulas is given in the following table.

| Data Type | Variable Declaration |
|-----------|---------------------|
| Number | NumberVar |

| Data Type | Variable Declaration |
|-----------|---------------------|
| String | StringVar |
| Date | DateVar |
| Date/Time | DateTimeVar |
| Currency | CurrencyVar |
| Time | TimeVar |

 **Access the Checklist tile on your CHOICE Course screen for reference information and job aids on How to Create a Manual Running Total.**

# ACTIVITY 1–4
## Creating a Manual Running Total on Detail Data

### Data File

C:\095203Data\Creating Running Totals\Manual RT Saddle Sales.rpt

### Before You Begin

The SAP Crystal Reports application is open.

### Scenario

You have a report that contains a running total field for calculating the sales volume, but you are not sure whether it's functioning properly. You want to create a manual running total to calculate the cumulative total of the sales volume and compare the results with the values generated by the existing running total field.

---

1. Create a formula for calculating the cumulative total of sales volume.
   a) Open the **Manual RT Saddle Sales.rpt** file.
   b) Switch to the **Design** view.
   c) In the **Field Explorer**, select **Formula Fields**, and then select the **New** button.
   d) In the **Name** text box, type *ManualRT* and then select **OK**.
   e) In the **Formula Workshop - Formula Editor - ManualRT** window, type *WhilePrintingRecords;* and press **Enter**.
   f) Continue to enter the formula to match the following:

   ```
   WhilePrintingRecords;
   NumberVar RunTotal;
   RunTotal := RunTotal + {Orders_Detail.Quantity}
   ```

   g) Check the formula for errors, and then select **Save and close**.

2. Place the formula in the report.
   a) In **Design** view, from the **Field Explorer**, drag the **ManualRT** formula to the 6-inch mark in the **Details** section.
   b) In the **PH** section, change the **ManualRT** label to *Manual Running Total* and then widen the label as needed to accommodate the text.
   c) Format the **Manual Running Total** label to match the formatting of the other labels.
   d) Preview the report.
   e) Verify that the manual running total displays the same results as the built-in Crystal Reports running total.
   f) Select the first manual running total field, and then select the **Decrease Decimals** button twice to remove the decimal digits from the field.
   g) Save the report as *My Manual RT Saddle Sales*
   h) Close the report.

---

# ACTIVITY 1–5
## Creating a Manual Running Total on Summary Data

**Data Files**

C:\095203Data\Creating Running Totals\Saddle Sales by Month.rpt

C:\095203Data\xtreme_B.mdb

**Before You Begin**

The SAP Crystal Reports application is open.

**Scenario**

You have a report that is grouped by month, displaying a quantity total for each month. You decide to calculate the cumulative total for the month quantity field and to group data for each calendar year. You also want to view the distribution of data for every month.

1. Create a formula for calculating the cumulative total for the month quantity field.
   a) Open the **Saddle Sales by Month.rpt** file.
   b) If necessary, switch to **Design** view.
   c) In the **Field Explorer**, select **Formula Fields**, and then select the **New** button.
   d) In the **Formula Name** dialog box, in the **Name** text box, type *ManualRT2* and then select **OK**.
   e) In the **Formula Workshop - Formula Editor - ManualRT2** window, in the **Function Tree**, expand **Evaluation Time**.
   f) Double-click **WhilePrintingRecords**, type *;* and press **Enter**.
   g) Continue the formula as follows:

   ```
   WhilePrintingRecords;
   NumberVar SumTotal :=SumTotal +
   ```

   h) In the **Field Tree**, expand **Report Fields** and double-click **Group #1: Orders.Order Date - A:Sum of Orders_Detail.Quantity**, which is the summary field for Group #1 that sums the quantity.
   i) Verify that your formula matches the following:

   ```
   WhilePrintingRecords;
   NumberVar SumTotal :=SumTotal + Sum ({Orders_Detail.Quantity},
   {Orders.Order Date}, "monthly")
   ```

   j) Check the formula for errors, and then select **Save and close**.
   k) On the **Insert** toolbar, select the **Insert Text Object** button, and in the **PH** section, click at the 2.5-inch mark so that the text object is placed in line with the other text objects.
   l) In the text object, type *Running Total* and click to the right of the text object to deselect it.

    **Note:** This text object will act as a heading for the running total you are going to insert in the **GH1** section.

2. Format the **Running Total** heading.
   a) In the **PH** section, select the **Quantity** text object to sample its formatting.
   b) On the **Standard** toolbar, select the **Format Painter** button, and then select the **Running Total** field heading to apply the formatting.
   c) Verify that the **Running Total** field heading now resembles the other text objects in the **PH** section.

    d) In the blue area of the **PH** section, right-click and select the **Select All Section Objects** option to select all three headings.

    e) Select **Format→Align→Tops** to arrange all text objects at the top of the **PH** section.

3. Place the **ManualRT2** formula in the **GH1** section and format the field.

    a) In the **Field Explorer**, select and drag the **ManualRT2** formula to the 2.5-inch mark in the **GH1** section.

    b) Preview the report.

    c) On the **Formatting** toolbar, select the **Decrease Decimals** button twice to decrease the decimal places by two points, and then switch to the **Design** view.

4. Display the cumulative totals for the month quantity fields for each calendar year.

    a) In the **Design** view, select **Insert→Group** to display the **Insert Group** dialog box.

    b) On the **Common** tab, from the first drop-down list, select **Orders.Order Date**.

    c) In the second drop-down list, verify that **in ascending order** is selected.

    d) In the **The section will be printed** section, from the drop-down list, select **for each year** to print the section for each year.

    e) Select **OK** to insert the group into the report.

    f) In the **Design** view, drag the **GH2** section to the **GH1** section so that the cumulative totals are displayed by year and then by month.

    g) Preview the report.

    h) Verify that the cumulative totals are now displayed for each month grouped for that specific calendar year.

5. Create a formula for resetting the running total field.

    a) Select the **Design** tab.

    b) In the **Field Explorer**, select **Formula Fields**, and then select the **New** button.

    c) In the **Formula Name** dialog box, in the **Name** text box, type *ResetRT* and then select **OK**.

    d) In the **Formula Workshop - Formula Editor - ResetRT** window, in the **Function Tree**, under **Evaluation Time**, double-click **WhilePrintingRecords**.

    e) Type *;* and press **Enter**.

    f) Complete the formula as follows:

```
WhilePrintingRecords;
NumberVar SumTotal :=0
```

    g) Check the formula for errors, and then select **Save and close**.

6. Display the cumulative totals for the month quantity field without taking into account the cumulative totals of the previous year.

    a) In the **Design** view, from the **Field Explorer**, drag the **ResetRT** formula field to the 2.5-inch mark in the **GH1** section.

    b) Right-click the **@ResetRT** formula and select **Format Field** to display the **Format Editor** dialog box.

    c) Select the **Common** tab, and then check the **Suppress** check box.

    d) Select **OK** to suppress the formula.

    e) Preview the report.

    f) Verify that the report now displays the cumulative totals for the month quantity fields without taking into account the cumulative totals of the previous year.

7. Create a formula for calculating the running total for each year.

    a) Select the **Design** tab.

    b) Create a new formula field called *ShowR*

    c) In the **Formula Workshop - Formula Editor - ShowR** window, in the **Function Tree**, under **Evaluation Time**, double-click **WhilePrintingRecords**.

    d) Type *;* and press **Enter**.

    e) Complete the formula as follows:

```
WhilePrintingRecords;
NumberVar SumTotal :=SumTotal;
```

    f)  Check the formula for errors, and then select **Save and close**.

8.  Create a heading for the **ShowR** formula.

    a)  On the **Insert** toolbar, select the **Insert Text Object** button, and then click in the **GF1** section at the 0-inch mark to place the new text object.

    b)  Type *Annual Total* and click outside the text object to deselect it.

    c)  Select the **Annual Total** text object.

>  **Note:** The **Annual Total** text object acts as a heading for the **ShowR** formula.

    d)  From the **Field Explorer**, drag the **ShowR** formula to the **GF1** section next to the **Annual Total** text object.

9.  Format the items in the group footer.

    a)  Position the mouse pointer over the line at the bottom of the **GF1** section and drag the double-headed arrow down by approximately half an inch.

    b)  On the **Insert** toolbar, select the **Insert Box** button, and then drag the mouse pointer around the objects in the **GF1** section to form a rectangle around the objects.

    c)  Select and drag all of the **GF1** section objects to the 1.5-inch mark so they align with the **Quantity** and **@ManualRT2** fields.

    d)  Preview the report.

    e)  Verify that the group footer section displays the cumulative total of the month quantity field for each year.

    f)  Deselect the items in the group footer section, and then select the first annual total field.

    g)  Select the **Decrease Decimals** button twice to remove the decimal places from the **ShowR** formula field.

    h)  Save the report as *My Saddle Sales by Month*

    i)  Close the report.

# Summary

In this lesson, you created and modified running totals manually and by using the built-in functionality of Crystal Reports. Creating running totals simplifies the task of tracking data incrementally.

**When will you use a running total field?**


**What are the advantages of using a running total?**

 **Note:** Check your CHOICE Course screen for opportunities to interact with your classmates, peers, and the larger CHOICE online community about the topics covered in this course or other topics you are interested in. From the Course screen you can also access available resources for a more continuous learning experience.

# 2 | Working with Cross-Tabs

**Lesson Time: 1 hour, 15 minutes**

## Lesson Objectives

In this lesson, you will:

- Create a cross-tab report.

- Format a cross-tab report.

- Create groups in cross-tab reports.

## Lesson Introduction

You created running totals to summarize data in your reports. Now, you want to summarize data based on multiple criteria.

You have a report in which data is grouped. Because the content spans several pages, you find it difficult to analyze the data. By using cross-tabs, you will be able to organize and analyze complex report data easily.

# TOPIC A

## Create a Cross-Tab Report

You created running totals to summarize data in your reports. A cross-tab is another feature you can use to summarize data in reports by displaying the data in a grid format.

A report may contain data that is retrieved from different tables, and the data may span several pages, making it difficult to comprehend. Creating a cross-tab allows you to present large amounts of data from different tables in a concise manner.

### Cross-Tabs

A *cross-tab* is a report presented in a column and row format that is used to summarize data. Rows in a cross-tab run horizontally, and columns run vertically. The intersection of a row and a column is called a *summarized field*. The value of a summarized field represents a total amount, such as a sum, count, or average of multiple values.

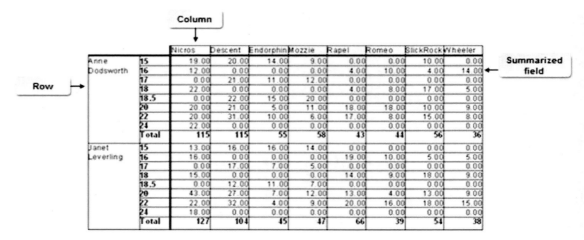

*Figure 2-1: A cross-tab displaying multiple records in a report.*

### Cross-Tab Components

A cross-tab consists of a number of components that help you display the required data in a report. The following table provides a description of each of the components.

| Component | Used To |
|---|---|
| **Row headings** | Specify the fields or formulas that will represent the row headings. |
| **Column headings** | Specify the fields or formulas that will represent the column headings. |
| **Grouping options** | Specify grouping options that you want to set for the row or column headings. For this, you need to determine if the data is in a format that will lend itself to this grouping easily. |
| **Data to be summarized** | Specify the data you need to summarize. |
| **Summary operation** | Specify the summary operation (sum, average, count) that you need for the summary fields. |

# The Cross-Tab Expert Dialog Box

The **Cross-Tab Expert** dialog box consists of three tabs that you can use to specify the settings for creating cross-tab reports.

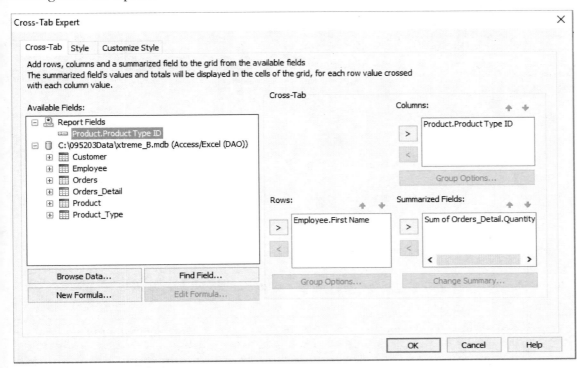

*Figure 2-2: The Cross-Tab Expert dialog box displaying fields in respective Cross-Tab list boxes.*

| Tab | Used To |
| --- | --- |
| **Cross-Tab** | Define a cross-tab report. The **Available Fields** section on this tab displays database fields. The **Cross-Tab** section is used to specify the settings for the rows, columns, and summarized fields of the cross-tab. |
| **Style** | Select a predefined style for a cross-tab report. A preview of the style is displayed on the tab. The **Custom style** option is used to apply custom settings to the report. |
| **Customize Style** | Create a custom style for a cross-tab report. In order to create and apply a custom style, on the **Style** tab, you must select the **Custom style** option. |

# The Cross-Tab Group Options Dialog Box

The **Cross-Tab Group Options** dialog box consists of the **Common** and **Options** tabs that you can use to sort and order data in a cross-tab report. You can use the **Common** tab to specify the database field to be used for grouping and can also specify the sort order. You can use the **Options** tab to specify the database field to be displayed in the group name field of the cross-tab.

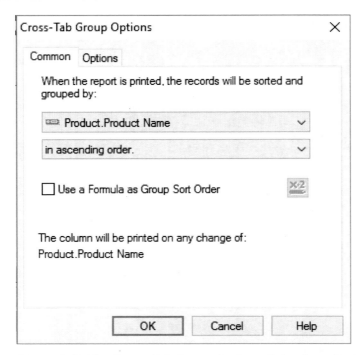

*Figure 2–3: The Cross–Tab Group Options dialog box displaying a selected field.*

 **Access the Checklist tile on your CHOICE Course screen for reference information and job aids on How to Create a Cross-Tab Report.**

# ACTIVITY 2–1
## Creating a Cross-Tab Report

### Data Files

C:\095203Data\Working with Cross-Tabs\2014-16 Bike Sales.rpt

C:\095203Data\xtreme_B.mdb

### Before You Begin

The Crystal Reports application is open.

### Scenario

You want to generate a report based on the quantity of bicycles sold by each employee. The report should also contain a breakdown of the quantity of the different bicycle models that an employee has sold.

---

1. Create a cross-tab with the product name as the column.
   a) Select the **Open File** link.
   b) In the **Open** dialog box, navigate to the **C:\095203Data\Working with Cross-Tabs** folder.
   c) Select the **2014-16 Bike Sales.rpt**, and then select **Open**.
   d) Switch to the **Design** view.
   e) On the **Insert** toolbar, select the **Insert Cross-Tab** button.
   f) In the **RHb** section, below the **Bicycles** text object, click to place the cross-tab.
   g) At the top-left corner of the cross-tab, right-click and select **Cross-Tab Expert**.
   h) In the **Cross-Tab Expert** dialog box, on the **Cross-Tab** tab, in the **Available Fields** list box, expand **Product** and select **Product Name**.
   i) Add the **Product Name** field to the **Columns** list box.

2. Display the first and last names of employees as row headings.
   a) In the **Available Fields** list box, expand **Employee**.
   b) Add the **First Name** field to the **Rows** list box, and then select **Group Options**.
   c) In the **Cross-Tab Group Options** dialog box, select the **Options** tab.
   d) Check the **Customize Group Name Field** check box.
   e) Select the **Use a Formula as Group Name** option, and then select the **Conditional Formula** button.
   f) If necessary, in the **Formula Workshop - Group Name Formula Editor** window, in the **Field Tree**, expand **C:\095203Data\xtreme_B.mdb (Access/Excel (DAO))**.
   g) In the **Field Tree**, expand **Employee**, and then double-click **First Name**.
   h) In the **Definition** area, type **+" "+**
   i) In the **Field Tree**, double-click **Last Name**.
   j) Compare your formula with the following:

      `{Employee.First Name}+" "+{Employee.Last Name}`
   k) Check the formula for errors, and then select **Save and close**.
   l) In the **Cross-Tab Group Options** dialog box, select **OK**.

3. Display order quantity as summarized fields.
   a) In the **Available Fields** list box, expand **Orders_Detail**.
   b) Add the **Quantity** field to the **Summarized Fields** list box.

4. Apply the **Original** formatting style to the cross-tab.
   a) Select the **Style** tab, and in the **Add style to the grid** list box, select **Original**, and then select **OK**.
   b) In the **Cross-Tab Expert** message box, select **Yes**.
   c) Preview the report.
   d) Verify that the report shows the breakdown in sales for each bike by each employee.
   e) In the cross-tab, select the second cell of the second row, and then select the **Decrease Decimals** button twice.
   f) Save the report as *My 2014-16 Bike Sales*

# TOPIC B

# Format a Cross-Tab Report

You created a cross-tab report. You want to enhance the aesthetic appeal of the cross-tab.

When you format text in a document, you make it easier for the audience to read. Similarly, when you format a cross-tab, you enhance the appearance and readability of the content.

## Formatting Options

The **Customize Style** tab in the **Cross-Tab Expert** dialog box displays options that you can use to format a cross-tab.

| Formatting Option | Used To |
|---|---|
| **Background Color** | Specify the background color for the row and column fields. |
| **Repeat Row Labels** | Include a row heading on each new page when a cross-tab does not fit on one page. |
| **Keep Columns Together** | Avoid page breaks within a column when a cross-tab does not fit on one page. |
| **Column Totals On Top/Row Totals On Left** | Change the placement of totals in a cross-tab. It positions the column totals at the top and row totals on the left. |
| **Show Cell Margins** | Add white space between the text and cell borders. Deselecting this option decreases the size of a cross-tab. |
| **Suppress Empty Rows/Suppress Empty Columns** | Hide the rows or columns that do not contain data. |
| **Suppress Row and/or Column Grand Totals** | Hide the row or column totals. This is particularly useful when a cross-tab does not contain both row and column headings. |
| **Format Grid Lines** | Separate multiple column or row headings from one another. It is also used to separate row and column headings from summary data, and controls the color, size, and suppression of grid lines. |
| **Indent Row Labels** | Specify the amount of indent for row labels. |
| **Indent Column Labels** | Specify the amount of indent for column labels. |

## The Format Editor Dialog Box

You can use the **Format Editor** dialog box to format the fields of a cross-tab report.

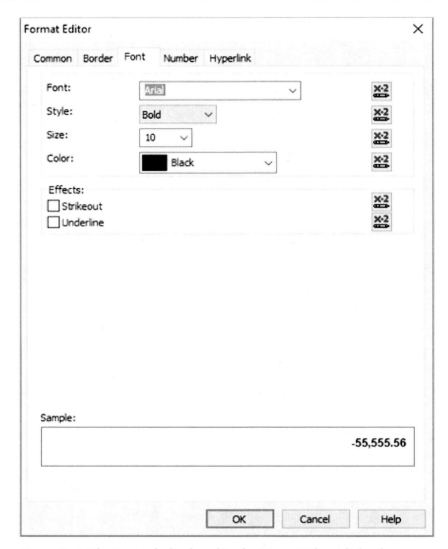

*Figure 2–4: The Font tab displayed in the Format Editor dialog box.*

The **Format Editor** dialog box tabs are described in the following table.

| Tab | Used To |
| --- | --- |
| **Common** | Specify settings for suppressing and aligning data. |
| **Border** | Format the borders of a field. A drop shadow, as well as a background color, can be applied to a border. |
| **Font** | Format the field text, including the font type, style, size, and color. |
| **Number** | Format the number style of a field. You can select from built-in styles or create a customized style. |
| **Hyperlink** | Create a hyperlink to a website, an email address, a file, a report object, or a drill-down. |

# The Highlighting Expert Dialog Box

You can use the **Highlighting Expert** dialog box to highlight the fields of a cross-tab report that meet specific criteria.

When used for conditional formatting, the **Highlighting Expert** dialog box allows you to:

- Modify several attributes at once, without writing a formula.
- Highlight all field types used in the report.
- Format font style, background color, font color, and border style.
- Format a field based on its own values or the values of another field.
- Highlight a cross-tab or Online Analytical Processing (OLAP) cell based on row and column heading values.
- Enter values using your locale-specific number format (such as 1,224.23 for North American users).
- Enter dates numerically or textually (January 12, 2001, or Jan 12, 2001).
- Undo highlighting quickly.

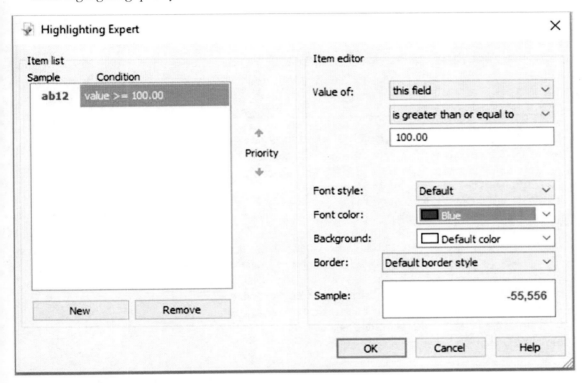

*Figure 2–5: The Highlighting Expert dialog box.*

## Aliases

You cannot use field names of cross-tab row and column headings directly in a formula. You must first assign a name to a row or column heading field in order to use it in a formula. After you assign a name, called an *alias*, the alias is displayed on the **Customize Style** tab of the **Cross-Tab Expert** dialog box. Then you can create formulas using the alias name rather than the field name.

 Access the Checklist tile on your **CHOICE Course** screen for reference information and job aids on **How to Format a Cross-Tab Report**.

# ACTIVITY 2-2
## Formatting a Cross-Tab Report

### Data File

C:\095203Data\xtreme_B.mdb

### Before You Begin

The My 2014-16 Bike Sales.rpt file is open.

### Scenario

You want the cross-tab report that you created to be visually appealing to your audience. You decide to format the report by highlighting the quantities sold by an employee when the quantity exceeds 100.

1. Format the cross-tab so that the grand total row is suppressed and the cross-tab is smaller.
    a) At the top-left corner of the cross-tab, right-click and select **Cross-Tab Expert**.
    b) Select the **Customize Style** tab, and in the **Grid Options** section, uncheck the **Show Cell Margins** check box.
    c) Check the **Suppress Row Grand Totals** check box.

2. Widen the gridlines for the borders.
    a) In the **Grid Options** section, select **Format Grid Lines**.
    b) In the **Format Grid Lines** dialog box, from the list box, select **Row labels right border**.
    c) In the **Line Options** section, from the **Width** drop-down list, select **1 pt**.
    d) In the list box, scroll down and select **Column label bottom border**.
    e) In the **Line Options** section, from the **Width** drop-down list, select **1 pt**.
    f) Select **OK** to close the **Format Grid Lines** dialog box.
    g) In the **Cross-Tab Expert** dialog box, select **OK**.

3. Resize the fields.
    a) In the **Preview** view, in the second row, select the second cell of the cross-tab.
    b) Drag the bottom-middle sizing handle down to increase the row height by twice its size.
    c) Switch to the **Design** view.

4. Create an alias for the column field.
    a) In the **Design** view, at the top-left corner of the cross-tab, right-click and select **Cross-Tab Expert**.
    b) In the **Cross-Tab Expert** dialog box, select the **Customize Style** tab.
    c) In the **Columns** list box, verify that **Product.Product Name** is selected.
    d) In the **Group Options** section, in the **Alias for Formulas** text box, select the default text and type *Pname* and then select **OK**.

5. Format the fields whose values are either greater than or equal to 100.
    a) In the cross-tab, at the intersection of the first row and the first column, right-click the **Detail.Quantity** field and select **Highlighting Expert**.
    Make sure you right-click the **Detail.Quantity** field in the first row and **not** in the **Total** row.
    b) In the **Highlighting Expert** dialog box, select **New**.
    c) In the **Item editor** area, in the **Value of** section, from the second drop-down list, select **is greater than or equal to**.

d) In the text box, type *100*
e) From the **Font color** drop-down list, select **Navy**.
f) From the **Background** drop-down list, select **Silver**.
g) Select **OK**.
h) Preview the report.
i) Verify that values equal to or exceeding 100 are displayed in the color navy against a silver background.
j) Save the report.

# TOPIC C

## Create Groups in Cross–Tab Reports

You formatted cross-tab reports to display data; however, the data may not be displayed in the desired order.

There may be times when you need to override a cross-tab's alphabetical sort to present data non-alphabetically. For example, if row headings represent countries in which you sell products, you may need to put a country ahead, regardless of its alphabetical order. Creating a specified group order allows you to group data to fit your needs.

### The Group Order

Group order is a method of grouping data in a cross-tab. You can specify the order by selecting the **in specified order** option in the **Cross-Tab Group Options** dialog box. You can also specify the values to be grouped by using the **Define Named Group** dialog box, which you can access from the **Specified Order** tab.

 Access the Checklist tile on your CHOICE Course screen for reference information and job aids on How to Create Groups in Cross-Tab Reports.

# ACTIVITY 2–3
## Creating Groups in Cross–Tab Reports

### Data File

C:\095203Data\xtreme_B.mdb

### Before You Begin

The My 2014-16 Bike Sales.rpt file is open.

### Scenario

The cross-tab report you created displays Nicros, Mini Nicros, and Micro Nicros as separate entries. You don't want them to be separate, because they are all the same products. Therefore, you decide to group them into a single entry. You also want a breakup of sales for every half year. Lastly, you want to change the report layout from portrait to landscape so all of the cross-tab columns appear on one page without being split over two pages.

1. Group all **Nicros** products.
   a) Select the **Design** tab.
   b) At the top-left corner of the cross-tab, right-click and select **Cross-Tab Expert**.
   c) In the **Cross-Tab Expert** dialog box, on the **Cross-Tab** tab, from the **Columns** list box, select **Product.Product Name**.
   d) Select **Group Options**.
   e) In the **Cross-Tab Group Options** dialog box, from the second drop-down list, select **in specified order**.
   f) On the **Specified Order** tab, select **New**.
   g) In the **Define Named Group** dialog box, in the **Group Name** text box, type *Nicros*
   h) On the **Product.Product Name** tab, from the drop-down list, select **is one of**.
   i) To the right of the drop-down list, in the text box, type *nicros*
   j) Select **Add**.
   k) Add the values *mini nicros* and *micro nicros*
   l) Select **OK**.
   m) In the **Cross-Tab Group Options** dialog box, select the **Others** tab, and then select the **Leave in their own groups** option.
   n) Select **OK**.
   o) In the **Cross-Tab Expert** dialog box, select **OK**.
   p) Preview the report.
   q) Verify that the **Nicros**, **Mini Nicros**, and **Micro Nicros** products are displayed under the **Nicros** group.

2. Group the data for every half year and ensure the groups aren't broken across pages.
   a) Select the **Design** tab.
   b) On the **Insert** toolbar, select the **Insert Group** button.
   c) In the **Insert Group** dialog box, in the first drop-down list, scroll down, and under **Orders**, select **Order Date**.
   d) In the **The section will be printed** area, from the drop-down list, select **for each half year**.
   e) Select the **Options** tab, and then select the **Keep Group Together** check box.
   f) In the **Insert Group** dialog box, select **OK**.

3. Display the report in groups.

a)  Drag the bottom sizing handle of the **GH1** section down to the top of the **PF** section to increase its size.

b)  Select the cross-tab object and drag it down to the **GH1** section, below the **Group #1: Order Date** object so that its left edge aligns with the left margin.

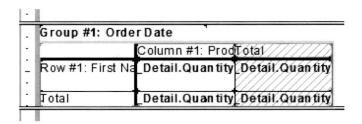

c)  Preview the report.

d)  In the **Groups** pane, select **July 2014** and verify that the cross-tabs are displayed for every half year.

4.  Change the report layout from portrait to landscape.

a)  Select **File→Page Setup**.

b)  In the **Page Setup** dialog box, in the **Page Options** section, in the **Orientation** area, select the **Landscape** option.

c)  Select **OK**.

d)  Preview the report and verify that the cross-tab columns appear on one page instead of being split over two pages.

e)  Save and close the report.

# Summary

In this lesson, you created a cross-tab in your report. Cross-tabs enable you to analyze complex data easily because the data is presented in a concise manner that makes it easy to compare information and identify trends.

**Which cross-tab components will help you display the required data in a report?**

**What kinds of data will you conditionally format in your cross-tabs?**

 **Note:** Check your CHOICE Course screen for opportunities to interact with your classmates, peers, and the larger CHOICE online community about the topics covered in this course or other topics you are interested in. From the Course screen you can also access available resources for a more continuous learning experience.

# 3 | Adding Subreports

**Lesson Time: 1 hour, 45 minutes**

## Lesson Objectives

In this lesson, you will:

- Insert a subreport.

- Edit a subreport.

- Share variables.

## Lesson Introduction

You created a cross-tab report to display complex data in rows and columns, and have split the output into separate reports. Now you need to organize data from different reports into a single report.

There may be instances when you must incorporate supplementary information from another report into your primary report. By creating subreports, you can display supplementary information within a primary report.

# TOPIC A

## Insert a Subreport

You worked with reports and used cross-tabs to perform calculations on data from a single report. The data may exist in separate reports that are unrelated or contain some linkable data.

There may be situations when you need to work on data that is logically split and stored in two different reports. For example, imagine A and B to be two different reports that are split logically. Instead of opening A and B every time, you can save time by inserting B as a subreport into A and accessing the data just by clicking the subreport link. By adding subreports, you will be able to correlate data from two reports.

## Subreports

A *subreport* is a report you can create when you want to correlate data from two unrelated reports, or data that cannot be linked by any other method. Subreports are placed within primary reports and have their own record selection criteria. They are inserted as objects in primary reports and should not be considered as primary reports themselves.

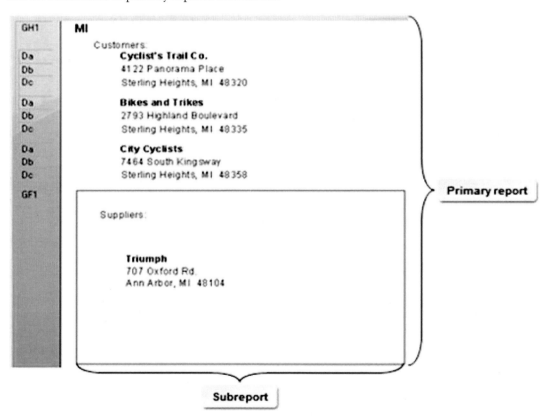

*Figure 3-1: A subreport inserted into a primary report.*

### The Structure of a Subreport

Subreports cannot include other subreports and do not contain page header or footer sections.

## Planning a Subreport

Before creating a subreport, you must determine the exact need for it and then decide on its components. The following table lists components that you need to consider when planning a subreport.

| Subreport Component | Helps You To |
|---|---|
| Data | Examine the data in both databases to see how it can be combined. |
| Location | Determine in which report section the subreport will be located. |
| Link fields | Determine the link fields, if any, that you will use. |
| Filter criteria | Determine the filter criteria, if any, that you need to incorporate in the subreport. |

### Multiple Subreports

You can add more than one subreport to a primary report by using the **Insert Subreport** dialog box.

# The Insert Subreport Dialog Box

The **Insert Subreport** dialog box consists of two tabs that have various options you can use to create subreports.

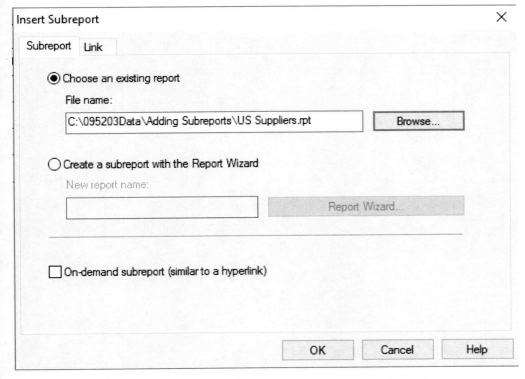

*Figure 3-2: The Subreport tab displayed in the Insert Subreport dialog box.*

| Tab | Description |
|---|---|
| **Subreport** | Enables you to insert subreports by selecting existing reports or creating new subreports using the **Report Wizard**. This tab contains the following three options: |
| | • The **Choose an existing report** option allows you to select an existing report as a subreport by either typing the file name directly in the **File name** text box or locating the file using the **Browse** button. |
| | • The **Create a subreport with the Report Wizard** option allows you to create a new subreport using the **Standard Report Creation Wizard**. |
| | • The **On-demand subreport** option, when enabled, displays subreport data only when you click the subreport hyperlink. |
| **Link** | Enables you to link data between the primary report and the subreport using common fields. |

 **Access the Checklist tile on your CHOICE Course screen for reference information and job aids on How to Insert a Subreport.**

# ACTIVITY 3–1
## Inserting a Subreport

### Data Files

C:\095203Data\Adding Subreports\US Customers.rpt

C:\095203Data\Adding Subreports\US Suppliers.rpt

C:\095203Data\xtreme_B.mdb

### Before You Begin

The Crystal Reports application is open.

### Scenario

You have a report that shows all the customers in the United States grouped by region. You have another report that has data about all the suppliers. The data sources for these reports are the **Customer** and **Supplier** tables in the xtreme_B.mdb database. You need to combine data from both reports into one report so the suppliers information appears in the appropriate region grouping beneath the customer list.

1. Make the **US Suppliers** report a subreport.
   a) Display the **Open** dialog box.
   b) Navigate to the **C:\095203Data\Adding Subreports** folder.
   c) Select the **US Customers.rpt** file, and then select **Open**.
   d) In the **Design** view, select **Insert→Subreport** to display the **Insert Subreport** dialog box.
   e) On the **Subreport** tab, select the **Choose an existing report** option, and then select **Browse**.
   f) In the **Open** dialog box, select the **US Suppliers.rpt** file, and then select **Open** to place the file name and pathway in the **File name** text box.

2. Link the subreport to the **Customer.Region** field and insert it in the first group footer.
   a) Select the **Link** tab.
   b) In the **Container Report field(s) to link to** section, in the **Available Fields** list box, select **Customer.Region** and add it to the **Field(s) to link to** list box as the field to be linked.
   c) In the **Customer.Region field link** section, verify that the **Select data in subreport based on field** check box is checked.
   d) Select **OK** to link the subreport to the main report.
   e) In the **GF1** section, click at the 0-inch mark to place the subreport.
   f) Verify that the **US Suppliers.rpt** file is added as a subreport.
   g) Preview the report.

3. Modify the line style of the subreport's border.
   a) Select the **US Suppliers.rpt** subreport.
   b) Select **Format→Format Subreport** to display the **Format Editor** dialog box.
   c) Select the **Border** tab.
   d) In the **Line style** section, change the **Left**, **Right**, **Top**, and **Bottom** border selections to **None**.
   e) Select **OK**.
   f) Click a blank area in the report to deselect the subreport.
      If no supplier information exists for a customer, the subreport data area is blank for that customer.
   g) Save the report as *My US Customers*

# TOPIC B

## Edit a Subreport

You inserted a subreport into a primary report. You find that the structure of the subreport doesn't match the primary report.

Viewing an improperly formatted subreport can be bothersome because users cannot comprehend the data easily. By editing a subreport, you can ensure that it appears the way you intend.

### The Re-import When Opening Option

You can use the **Re-import When Opening** option to update the subreport in a primary report with a new copy of the subreport in the original location. If you make changes to the embedded subreport, you need to uncheck the **Re-import When Opening** check box to avoid losing the changes when the primary report is opened later.

 **Note:** The **Re-import When Opening** option works properly only when the subreport is at the same location in the primary report as it was originally inserted.

### On-Demand Subreports

An *on-demand subreport* appears as a link in a primary report. To improve report performance, the subreport data is retrieved from its source only when a user clicks the link. The data of an on-demand subreport is displayed on a separate **Preview** tab.

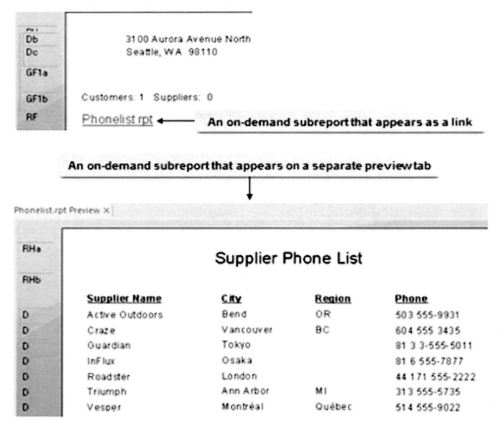

*Figure 3-3: An on-demand subreport called by the primary report.*

**Note:** The on-demand subreport is always displayed at the end of a primary report in the form of a link.

 **Access the Checklist tile on your CHOICE Course screen for reference information and job aids on How to Edit a Subreport.**

# ACTIVITY 3–2
## Editing a Subreport

### Data File

C:\095203Data\xtreme_B.mdb

### Before You Begin

The My US Customers.rpt file is open.

### Scenario

You have a primary report with a subreport inserted. You are planning to submit the report to your manager after adding some final touches to it. You want to display the subreport data only when there are suppliers, and you want the subreport to be updated the next time you open it.

---

1. Delete extra sections in the subreport.
   a) Select the **Design** tab.
   b) Right-click the **US Suppliers.rpt** subreport and select **Edit Subreport** to display the subreport.
   c) In the blue area of the **RFb** section, right-click and select **Delete Section** to delete it.
   d) Select **View→Print Preview**.
   e) In the **Enter Values** dialog box, in the **Pm-Customer.Region** text box, type **MI** as the customer region, and then select **OK**.
   f) Verify that the **US Suppliers.rpt Preview** tab displays one supplier for the **MI** region.

2. Import the subreport when the primary report is opened and also suppress it when there are no records.
   a) Switch to the **Design** view.
   b) Right-click the **US Suppliers.rpt** subreport and select **Format Subreport**.
   c) In the **Format Editor** dialog box, select the **Subreport** tab.
   d) On the **Subreport** tab, check the **Re-import When Opening** check box.
   e) Check the **Suppress Blank Subreport** check box, and then select **OK**.

3. Suppress blank sections in the report.
   a) In the blue area of the **GF1** section, right-click and select **Section Expert**.
   b) In the **Section Expert** dialog box, on the **Common** tab, check the **Suppress Blank Section** check box to suppress sections that are blank, and then select **OK**.
   c) Select **View→Print Preview** to preview the changes in the subreport.
   d) Verify that the group footer of the report now displays only subreports that have data.
   e) Save the report and close the file.

---

# ACTIVITY 3-3
## Creating an On-Demand Subreport

## Data Files

C:\095203Data\xtreme_B.mdb

C:\095203Data\Adding Subreports\Contacts.rpt

C:\095203Data\Adding Subreports\Phonelist.rpt

## Before You Begin

The Crystal Reports application is open.

## Scenario

You created a report that has a list of names and addresses of customers and suppliers. You're planning to include a list of suppliers' phone numbers at the end of the report. You want the subreport to appear as a link so you can view the phone information only when you need it.

1. Add an on-demand subreport to the footer of the primary report.
   a) Open the **Contacts.rpt** file.
   b) In the **Design** view, select **Insert→Subreport** to open the **Insert Subreport** dialog box.
   c) On the **Subreport** tab, select the **Choose an existing report** option, and then select **Browse** to search for a report.
   d) In the **Open** dialog box, open the **Phonelist.rpt** file.
   e) Check the **On-demand subreport (similar to a hyperlink)** check box, and then select **OK**.
   f) In the **RF** section, click at the 0-inch mark to place the subreport.
   g) Verify that the subreport is now displayed as a hyperlink.

2. Format the on-demand subreport to include an on-demand subreport caption and a subreport preview tab caption.
   a) Right-click the **Phonelist.rpt** subreport link and select **Format Subreport**.
   b) In the **Format Editor** dialog box, select the **Subreport** tab.
   c) To the right of the **On-demand Subreport Caption**, select the **Conditional Formula** button to assign a formula.
   d) In the **Formula Workshop - Format Formula Editor - On-Demand Subreport Caption** window, in the **Definition** area, type a formula to add the caption *Supplier Phone List* to the on-demand subreport.

    **Note:** Remember to add quotation marks around the caption text.

   e) Check the formula for errors, and then select **Save and close**.
   f) In the **Format Editor** dialog box, to the right of the **Subreport Preview Tab Caption**, select the **Conditional Formula** button.
   g) In the **Formula Workshop - Format Formula Editor - Subreport Preview Caption** window, in the **Definition** area, type a formula to add the caption *Phone List* to the subreport preview.
   h) Check the formula for errors, and then select **Save and close**.
   i) In the **Format Editor** dialog box, select **OK**.

3. Test the on-demand subreport.
   a) Preview the report.
   b) On the **Navigation** toolbar, click the **Show Next Page** button to advance to the next page.

c) Click the **Supplier Phone List** link to display the on-demand subreport.

d) Verify that the subreport is displayed on a new preview tab with the caption you created earlier.

e) Save the report as *My Contacts* and close the file.

# TOPIC C

# Share Variables

You edited a subreport. At times, you may want to pass data back and forth between primary reports and subreports.

Summaries are often presented at the end of reports, and it's common to display information from subreports in those summaries. By sharing variables between subreports and primary reports, you will be able to apply the results from a subreport formula to the primary report.

## The Count Function

The *Count* function enables you to count the values that appear in a report for a specified field. For example, the following function returns a count of records in the **Customer** table for each region in which the **Customer Name** field is completed: **Count ({Customer.Customer Name}, {Customer.Region})**. If the **Customer Name** field is not completed, it is not included in the count.

### Null

You might commonly use the **Count** function to determine whether a subreport returns a certain number of records. If no records are found in the subreport, the Count function returns a *null* value rather than a zero.

## Shared Variables

A *shared variable* is a type of variable that Crystal Reports provides that enables you to pass data back and forth between primary reports and subreports. You must create a formula in both the primary report and the subreport that declares the same shared variable. One of the formulas must assign a value to the shared variable. A shared variable can also pass data back and forth between one subreport to another.

>  **Note:** In order for Crystal Reports to consider two variable declarations to be the same variable, they must have the same name and data type because the Crystal Reports syntax is not case-sensitive.

Primary Report Formula — **Shared variable**

```
Shared NumberVar SupplyCnt;
"Customers: " & Count ({Customer.Customer Name},
{Customer.Region}) & " Suppliers: " & SupplyCnt
```

**Shared variable**

Subreport Formula

**Value assigned to the shared variable**

```
WhilePrintingRecords;
Shared NumberVar SupplyCnt;
If IsNull (Count ({Supplier.Supplier Name}))
Then SupplyCnt := 0
Else SupplyCnt := Count ({Supplier.Supplier Name})
```

*Figure 3–4: Shared variable.*

## Variable Scope

*Variable scope* defines the degree to which variables in one formula are made available to other formulas.

| Scope Type | Extent of Availability of the Variable Content |
|---|---|
| Global | Variable contents are available for the entire report. Example:<br>`Global StringVar MyVar;`<br><br>**Note:** Use of the word `Global` is optional. All variables are global by default when using the Crystal Reports syntax. |
| Local | Variable contents are available only within the formula in which they are created. Example:<br>`Local StringVar MyVar;` |
| Shared | Variable contents are available for the entire report and any subreports. Example:<br>`Shared StringVar MyVar;` |

## The Section Expert Dialog Box

You can use the **Section Expert** dialog box to format entire sections of your report. By selecting a section of a report in the **Section Expert** dialog box, you can view and set formatting properties for the section. Depending on which section you select, properties will vary and some will not be available. The **Suppress Blank Section** option suppresses all blank objects inside an entire section. This is useful in situations in which you want to avoid white gaps in the report.

 Access the Checklist tile on your CHOICE Course screen for reference information and job aids on How to Share Variables.

# ACTIVITY 3-4
## Sharing Formulas Between Primary Reports and Subreports

### Data Files

C:\095203Data\xtreme_B.mdb

C:\095203Data\Adding Subreports\My US Customers.rpt

### Before You Begin

The Crystal Reports application is open.

### Scenario

You have a report that lists customers and suppliers within each region. You want to include a summary statement that displays the total number of customers and suppliers in each region.

1. Create a formula in the subreport that can be shared with the primary report.
   a) Open the **My US Customers.rpt** file.
   b) In the **Design** view, double-click the **US Suppliers.rpt** subreport to display the subreport.
   c) Begin creating a formula called *SuppliersCount*
   d) In the **Formula Workshop - Formula Editor - SuppliersCount** window, in the **Definition** area, enter the following formula for counting the number of suppliers in each region:

   ```
   WhilePrintingRecords;
   Shared NumberVar SupplyCnt; If IsNull (Count ({Supplier.Supplier Name}))
   Then SupplyCnt:= 0
   Else SupplyCnt:= Count ({Supplier.Supplier Name})
   ```

   e) Check the formula for errors, and then select **Save and close**.
   f) From the **Field Explorer**, select and drag the **SuppliersCount** formula to the 0-inch mark in the **RF** section.

2. Suppress the subreport's footer.
   a) On the **Experts** toolbar, select the **Section Expert** button to display the **Section Expert** dialog box.
   b) In the left pane, select **Report Footer** as the section to be suppressed.
   c) On the **Common** tab, check the **Suppress (No Drill-Down)** check box to suppress the section, and then select **OK**.
   d) Select **View→Print Preview**.
   e) In the **Enter Values** dialog box, in the **Pm-Customer.Region** text box, type *MI* and then select **OK**.

3. Create a formula in the primary report that displays the number of customers and suppliers available in each state.
   a) In the primary report, in the **Design** view, create a formula named *SummaryText*
   b) In the **Formula Workshop - Formula Editor - SummaryText** window, in the **Definition** area, enter the following formula that calculates the number of customers and suppliers in each state:

   ```
   Shared NumberVar SupplyCnt;
   "Customers: " & Count ({Customer.Customer Name}, {Customer.Region}) &
   "Suppliers: " & SupplyCnt
   ```

   c) Check the formula for errors, and then select **Save and close**.

4. Place the **SupplierText** formula in a new group footer.

   a) In the blue area of the **GF1** section, right-click and select **Insert Section Below** to insert a new group footer.

   b) From the **Field Explorer**, select and drag the **SummaryText** formula to the 0-inch mark in the **GF1b** section.

   c) Preview the report.

   d) Verify that a count for each of the customers and suppliers is displayed in the report.

   e) Save and close the report.

# Summary

In this lesson, you inserted a subreport into a primary report. By adding a subreport, you correlated data from two reports with some linkable data.

**Under what circumstances will you add a subreport?**

**What scopes will you generally use when declaring a shared variable?**

 **Note:** Check your CHOICE Course screen for opportunities to interact with your classmates, peers, and the larger CHOICE online community about the topics covered in this course or other topics you are interested in. From the Course screen you can also access available resources for a more continuous learning experience.

# 4 | Creating Drill-Downs in a Report

**Lesson Time: 1 hour, 5 minutes**

## Lesson Objectives

In this lesson, you will:

- Create a drill-down.
- Create headings for drill-down data.

## Lesson Introduction

You created subreports to be displayed along with a primary report. Instead of displaying detailed data in the primary report, you may want to display only the summary information.

You have a large report containing sales information, and you don't want the data to be displayed all at once. You want to display only the summary values initially so that people viewing your report can see important data. By creating a drill-down, you will be able to display detailed data on which any given summary is based.

# TOPIC A

## Create a Drill-Down

You created subreports in a primary report to display related data. You now want to display the data only on request.

You are creating a report to display the total salary expenses for each department in your company. Although you want the report to display only the summary of the salary expense for each department, you also want the detailed data on which the summary data is based to be accessible. By creating a drill-down, you will be able to easily scan the report to view the total salary expense amount for each department and then drill down to view the detailed salary expenses within each department.

## Drill-Downs

A *drill-down* is a feature that allows you to view detailed information about summarized data. The detailed data, also referred to as the drill-down data, is displayed only when you request it. A report can contain several levels of drill-downs. You can also implement a drill-down for charts and maps.

 **Note:** There are two methods of drilling down data: expanded and focused. In an expanded drill-down, you access the data by clicking the plus symbol next to the summary data. In a focused drill-down, you access the data by double-clicking the summary data.

 **Access the Checklist tile on your CHOICE Course screen for reference information and job aids on How to Create a Drill-Down.**

# ACTIVITY 4–1
## Creating a Drill-Down

## Data Files

C:\095203Data\xtreme_B.mdb

C:\095203Data\Creating Drill-Downs\Customer Sales Total.rpt

## Before You Begin

The Crystal Reports application is open.

## Scenario

You want to present a report for documenting the sales achievement in your organization. In addition to including the total sales made to each customer in the primary report, you may want to display data for an individual sale.

1. Summarize and group the report data.
   a) Display the **Open** dialog box.
   b) Navigate to the **C:\095203Data\Creating Drill-Downs** folder.
   c) Select the **Customer Sales Total.rpt** file, and then select **Open**.
   d) On the **Insert** toolbar, select the **Insert Summary** button. $\Sigma$
   e) In the **Insert Summary** dialog box, in the **Choose the field to summarize** drop-down list, scroll down, and in the **Orders** table, select **Order Amount**.
   f) In the **Calculate this summary** drop-down list, verify that **Sum** is selected.
   g) In the **Summary location** section, select **Insert Group** to create a group in which the summary data will be stored.
   h) In the **Insert Group** dialog box, from the first drop-down list, select **Customer Name**, and then select **OK**.
   i) In the **Insert Summary** dialog box, select **OK**.
   j) Select the **Design** tab.
   k) Drag the summary data object from the **GF1** section to the 2-inch mark in the **GH1** section.

2. Add more fields to the report.
   a) In the **Field Explorer**, expand **Database Fields**, and then expand the **Customer** table.
   b) Drag the **Customer Name** field to the 0-inch mark in the **Details** section.
   c) In the **Field Explorer**, expand **Orders** and drag the **Order Date** field to the 3.5-inch mark in the **Details** section.
   d) From the **Field Explorer**, drag the **Order Amount** field to the left of the **Order Date** field at the 2-inch mark in the **Details** section.

3. Format the **Order Date** field.
   a) In the **Details** section, right-click the **Order Date** field and select **Format Field**.
   b) In the **Format Editor** dialog box, on the **Date and Time** tab, in the **Style** list box, select **03/01/1999**, and then select **OK**.
   c) Preview the report.
   d) Verify that the customer name is displayed twice.

4. Hide the drill-down data for the primary report.
   a) On the **Experts** toolbar, select the **Section Expert** button.

    b) In the **Section Expert** dialog box, in the **Sections** list box, select **Details**.

    c) On the **Common** tab, check the **Hide (Drill-Down OK)** check box, and then select **OK**.

5. View the drill-down data.

    a) Place the mouse pointer over the summary data for **Alley Cat Cycles** and notice that the mouse pointer changes to a magnifying glass.

        Alley Cat Cycles 🔍                                           $54,565.39

    b) Double-click **Alley Cat Cycles** to view the drill-down data.

    c) Verify that the summary data for **Alley Cat Cycles** is displayed at the top of the page and the individual records are now displayed for each date.

    d) Close the **Alley Cat Cycles** tab.

    e) Save the report as *My Customer Sales Total*

# TOPIC B

# Create Headings for Drill–Down Data

You created drill-downs in a report. Now, you may want to display headings for each drill-down level to differentiate one level from another.

Imagine having a report that has multiple levels of drill-down and you need to present the data in a meeting. The audience might find it difficult to locate the appropriate information because of the levels of drill-down. By creating headings for the drill-down data, you will be able to display a heading for each drill-down level, thereby making it easier for the audience to comprehend.

## The DrillDownGroupLevel Function

You can use the **DrillDownGroupLevel** function to identify each drill-down level numerically within formulas. While the primary report displaying the summary data can be identified using the formula **DrillDownGroupLevel = 0**, the first drill-down level can be identified using the formula **DrillDownGroupLevel = 1**. You can also use the **DrillDownGroupLevel** function to suppress a particular report section when the specified drill-down level is viewed.

> **Access the Checklist tile on your CHOICE Course screen for reference information and job aids on How to Create Headings for Drill-Down Data.**

# ACTIVITY 4–2
## Creating Headings for Drill–Down Data

### Data File

C:\095203Data\xtreme_B.mdb

### Before You Begin

The My Customer Sales Total.rpt file is open.

### Scenario

The sales report is almost finished; however, the drill-down data doesn't have any headings, so it appears incomplete. Also, the headings in the different levels must appear only in their respective levels.

---

1. Create a **Group Header** section for drill-down headings.
   a) On the **Preview** tab, verify that the **Order Date** and **Order Amount** field headings are displayed.
   b) Select the **Design** tab.
   c) In the blue area of the **GH1** section, right-click and select **Insert Section Below**.
   d) In the blue area of the **PH** section, right-click and select the **Select All Section Objects** option.
   e) Press the **Down Arrow** key twice to move the three selected items to the **GH1b** section.

2. Suppress the drill-down heading for the primary report.
   a) Display the **Section Expert** dialog box.
   b) In the **Section Expert** dialog box, in the **Sections** list box, select **Group Header #1b: Customer.Customer Name - A**, and then select the **Conditional Formula** button to the right of the **Suppress (No Drill-Down)** check box.

   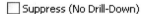 

   c) In the **Formula Workshop - Format Formula Editor - Suppress (No Drill-Down)** window, in the **Definition** area, enter the following formula to suppress the section for the primary report:

   `DrillDownGroupLevel=0`
   d) Check the formula for errors, and then select **Save and close**.
   e) In the **Section Expert** dialog box, select **OK**.
   f) Preview the report.
   g) Verify that the **Order Date** and **Order Amount** field headings are not displayed.

3. Add the heading "Customer Sales Totals" to the summary data.
   a) Select the **Design** tab.
   b) On the **Insert** toolbar, select the **Insert Text Object** button.
   c) In the **PH** section, click at the 0-inch mark to insert a text object.
   d) Type *Customer Sales Totals* and click to the right of the text object to deselect the object.
   e) Select the **Customer Sales Totals** text object.
   f) On the **Formatting** toolbar, from the **Font Size** drop-down list, select **12**.
   g) On the **Formatting** toolbar, select the **Bold** button.
   h) Drag the middle-right sizing handle of the text object to the 2-inch mark.

    i)   Drag the bottom-middle sizing handle down to increase the size of the text object to twice its original size.

    j)   Drag the bottom sizing handle of the **GH1b** section down to the top of the **GF1** section.

**4.**  Format the summary heading and suppress it in the drill-down report.

    a)   In the **GH1a** section, select the **Group #1: Customer Name** field.

    b)   On the **Formatting** toolbar, select the **Bold** button.

    c)   Display the **Section Expert** dialog box.

    d)   In the **Sections** list box, select **Group Header #1a: Customer.Customer Name - A**, and to the right of the **Suppress (No Drill-Down)** check box, select the **Conditional Formula** button.

    e)   In the **Formula Workshop - Format Formula Editor - Suppress (No Drill-Down)** window, type the following code to suppress the **GH1a** section for the first drill-down level:

```
DrillDownGroupLevel=1
```

    f)   Check the formula for errors, and then select **Save and close**.

    g)   In the **Section Expert** dialog box, select **OK**.

    h)   Preview the report.

    i)   Verify that the heading **Customer Sales Totals** is displayed in the report.

    j)   Drill down to view the details for **Alley Cat Cycles**.

    k)   Verify that the heading **Customer Sales Totals** is **not** displayed, and the **Customer Name, Order Amount**, and **Order Date** column headings **are** displayed.

    l)   Close the **Alley Cat Cycles** tab.

    m)  Save and close the report.

# Summary

In this lesson, you created drill-downs in a report. Using drill-downs, you displayed detailed data on which summaries were based.

**Depict a few situations where you will use drill-down reports.**


**How will the DrillDownGroupLevel function help you in Crystal Reports?**

 **Note:** Check your CHOICE Course screen for opportunities to interact with your classmates, peers, and the larger CHOICE online community about the topics covered in this course or other topics you are interested in. From the Course screen you can also access available resources for a more continuous learning experience.

# 5 | Using SQL Statements in Report Processing

**Lesson Time: 2 hours, 10 minutes**

## Lesson Objectives

In this lesson, you will:

- Create a report using SQL queries.

- Summarize report data.

- Create joins using SQL.

- Create subqueries.

- Create an SQL expression field.

## Lesson Introduction

You created drill-downs in a report to access detailed data on request. As you work with larger and more complex reports, the tools provided by SAP® Crystal Reports® may not be sufficient to meet all of your data needs.

Reports that contain complex data may take a lot of time to load. By writing queries using SQL statements, you will not only be able to create reports that contain the desired data, but also increase report performance.

# TOPIC A

## Create a Report Using SQL Queries

You created drill-downs in a report to view detailed data only when requested. After viewing the data in the report, you find that some of the required data is not present.

There might be situations when you need to locate specific information in a report that has thousands of records. Manually locating the required information would be time-consuming and cumbersome. Writing SQL queries within Crystal Reports increases report performance because data is processed more efficiently.

### Server-Side Processing

*Server-side processing* is a report-processing technique that is carried out on the remote server containing the database, rather than on the client computer. Server-side processing works for reports that need to be sorted, filtered, grouped, or totaled, and for reports based on SQL data sources. It also enables you to pass relevant details onto the client system, thus taking less time and local memory.

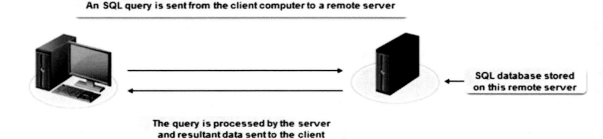

**An SQL query is sent from the client computer to a remote server**

**SQL database stored on this remote server**

**The query is processed by the server and resultant data sent to the client**

*Figure 5-1: Server-side processing.*

### Factors Affecting Server-Side Processing

Some aspects of a report can prohibit or restrict the amount of processing that can be done on a server. In an ideal world, all record selection, sorting, grouping, and totaling operations would be done at the server level. However, some of the most valuable features in Crystal Reports result in situations in which processing can't be done on the server. In some cases, only partial server processing may be possible. Reports with drill-down capability, running totals with variables, specified grouping, or Crystal Reports functions are just a few examples of the factors that inhibit server-side processing. Specifying report tasks using SQL can greatly enhance the likelihood that processing will occur on the server.

### SQL

*Structured Query Language (SQL)* is the standard query language used within other programming languages or applications to access and manipulate relational database data. When using Crystal Reports to access data from SQL and Open Database Connectivity (ODBC) database sources, most of the data manipulation you specify is automatically converted by Crystal Reports to SQL statements. In addition, you can manually write SQL statements within Crystal Reports.

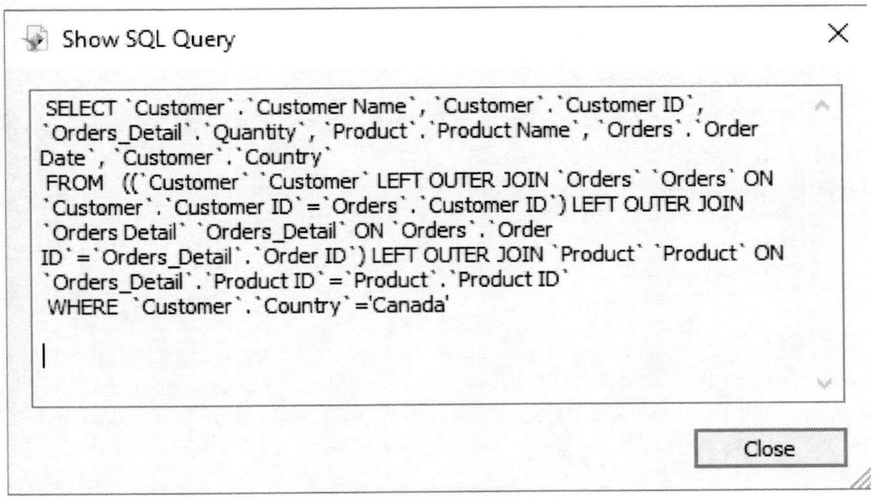

*Figure 5-2: An SQL statement displayed in the dialog box.*

## SQL Clauses

*SQL clauses* are the components of an SQL statement that you can use to indicate the task you want the database to perform.

| Clause | Description |
|---|---|
| **SELECT** | Indicates the names of the fields whose data you want to retrieve. This clause is mandatory in an SQL statement. |
| **FROM** | Indicates the table containing the field data you want to retrieve. This clause is mandatory in an SQL statement. |
| **WHERE** | Sets the record filter criteria. This clause is optional. |
| **GROUP BY** | Establishes grouping. This clause is optional. |
| **HAVING** | Sets the group filter criteria. It filters data retrieved by **GROUP BY** and displays data only when the retrieved aggregate values suit the conditions specified in this clause. It is used only in conjunction with the **GROUP BY** clause. |
| **ORDER BY** | Determines the sort order. This clause is optional. |

### The DISTINCT Keyword

When the **DISTINCT** keyword appears within the **SELECT** clause, it indicates that only unique data values will be retrieved, without the names being duplicated. For example, the following SQL statement will retrieve only one instance of each customer name from the **Purchases** table, even though it may contain more than one instance of a customer name.

```
SELECT DISTINCT custname
FROM Purchases
```

## SQL Statements

An *SQL statement* is a request that is written using SQL clauses. It's sent to a server containing an SQL database for performing specific database tasks. You can use SQL statements to create a database file, add tables and fields to a database, add records to tables, or retrieve data from databases.

SELECT Region, Count(Customer.`Customer ID`)
AS `Number of Customers`
FROM Customer
GROUP By Region
ORDER By Region

SQL clauses

SQL statement

*Figure 5-3: An example of an SQL statement.*

### The Asterisk (*) Character

When the * character appears following the **SELECT** clause keyword, the SQL statement will retrieve all fields in the specified table. For example, the following SQL query will retrieve all fields from the **Orders** table. When you want to retrieve all fields in a table, using the * character saves you from having to type the names of all the fields.

```
SELECT *
FROM Orders
```

> **Note:** SQL is not a true computer language, and can't be used to create stand-alone applications.

## SQL Rules

You need to follow certain rules while using SQL statements to retrieve data in Crystal Reports.

- The clauses that you use must always appear in the following order: **SELECT, FROM, WHERE, GROUP BY, HAVING, ORDER BY**.
- You must type a space after each clause keyword.
- You have to ensure that, in table and field names that include multiple words, each word is separated by a space entered within grave characters, quotation characters, or brackets [ ].
- If a referenced field uses a name that is also used by fields in other tables within the database, you must precede the field name with the table name and a period.

### SQL Query Example

You are the CEO of an organization. You decide to create a report that contains the details of employees from each department who were born after 1970 and have a present biweekly salary greater than US $3,500. You need to write an SQL query to retrieve the desired data. The given query starts with the **SELECT** clause and ends with the **WHERE** clause. Each database field is separated using a comma. You should insert a space between each clause, and separate each field by the grave character.

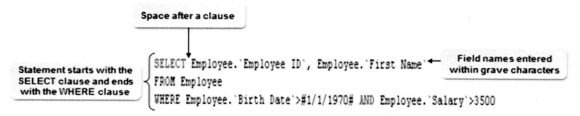

Space after a clause

Statement starts with the
SELECT clause and ends
with the WHERE clause

SELECT Employee.`Employee ID`, Employee.`First Name`
FROM Employee
WHERE Employee.`Birth Date`>#1/1/1970# AND Employee.`Salary`>3500

Field names entered
within grave characters

*Figure 5-4: Example of SQL query.*

### Acronyms

Some people find the acronym **SoFtWareGHOst** helpful as a reminder for the correct order of the clauses. The uppercase characters in the acronym represent the query clauses.

## The Grave Character

The grave character (`` ` ``), also known as a back tick, is typically located to the left of the **1** key. A report generated from a Microsoft® Access® connection uses the grave mark, so in this case, quotation marks would not be interpreted correctly if they are located around field or table names containing spaces. When Crystal Reports generates SQL statements based on Crystal Reports commands that you specify, the grave or quotation characters are added automatically to field and table names, regardless of whether the names include spaces.

## SQL Conventions

Certain SQL conventions are not required, but should be followed to ensure your Crystal Reports SQL queries are clear and effective. The following table describes the most common SQL conventions.

| Convention | Example |
|---|---|
| Clause keywords should appear in uppercase characters so they are easily distinguishable among the other components of the statement. | `SELECT Position, `Supervisor ID`` <br> `FROM Employee` |
| Each clause should appear on its own line to keep the statement from becoming confusing to read. | `SELECT Orders.Amount` <br> `FROM Orders` |

## SQL Items Automatically Generated by Crystal Reports

When you view the SQL statement automatically generated by Crystal Reports based on the commands specified by the user, it may look different from the one you have created to achieve the same result. Crystal Reports may add several items to the automatically generated SQL as necessary.

The following table describes the reasons for such additions.

| SQL Item Generated in Crystal Reports | Reason for Using This Component | Example |
|---|---|---|
| All field names may appear preceded by the table name, with a period separating the table and field name. | This is useful to add clarity to your SQL statements when you are accessing a database that includes many tables, and is required when you are accessing a field whose name matches another field name used in a different table. | `SELECT Contact.Name` <br> `FROM Contact` |
| Field, table, and other object names may be enclosed within grave or quotation marks. The character generated by the Microsoft Access connection is a grave mark. | These special enclosing grave or quotation marks are required only when object names include spaces. Using them is considered poor style in database design, so they are rarely used. The Crystal Reports generator adds these characters to all fields and tables, whether or not they use a space. | `SELECT `Income`.`1st Qtr`` <br> `FROM `Income`` |

| SQL Item Generated in Crystal Reports | Reason for Using This Component | Example |
|---|---|---|
| In the **FROM** clause, the table name appears twice. | The second instance of the table name is actually an alias. Crystal Reports automatically specifies an alias name for all report tables, which, by default, matches the name of the original table. An alias is often created to provide a shorter name that can be used throughout the statement in place of the original table name. | SELECT `Contact`.`Name` FROM `Income` `Income` |

 **Note:** To explore how to customize reports, access the Spotlight on **Using Case Statements** presentation from the **Spotlight** tile on the CHOICE course screen.

 **Access the Checklist tile on your CHOICE Course screen for reference information and job aids on How to Create a Report Using SQL Queries.**

# ACTIVITY 5-1
## Creating a Report Using an SQL Query

### Data File
C:\095203Data\xtreme_B.mdb

### Before You Begin
The Crystal Reports application is open.

### Scenario
You want to generate a report that displays the name of each employment position in your company's sales department alphabetically, along with the supervisor ID for the person who oversees each position. The data is present in the **xtreme_B.mdb** database. You want to begin entering SQL manually to generate reports, but you are not sure that you could do so correctly.

---

1. Create a report that displays the supervisor ID and position.
   a) Select the **Blank report** link.
   b) In the **Database Expert** dialog box, in the **Available Data Sources** list box, expand **C:\095203Data \xtreme_B.mdb**.
   c) Expand **Tables** and select **Employee**.
   d) Add **Employee** to the **Selected Tables** list box, and then select **OK**.
   e) In the **Field Explorer**, expand **Database Fields**, and then expand **Employee**.
   f) From the **Field Explorer**, drag the **Position** field to the 0-inch mark in the **Details** section.
   g) Drag the **Supervisor ID** field to the 2-inch mark in the **Details** section.
   h) Preview the report.
   i) Verify that the report displays the employee positions in the organization, along with their supervisor ID.

| Position | Supervisor ID |
|---|---|
| Sales Representative | 5 |
| Vice President, Sales | |
| Sales Representative | 5 |
| Sales Representative | 5 |
| Sales Manager | 2 |
| Sales Representative | 5 |
| Sales Representative | 5 |
| Inside Sales Coordinator | 5 |
| Sales Representative | 5 |
| Business Manager | 2 |
| Mail Clerk | 10 |
| Receptionist | 10 |
| Marketing Director | 2 |
| Marketing Associate | 13 |
| Advertising Specialist | 13 |

2. Sort the data by the **Position** field in ascending order.
   a) On the **Experts** toolbar, select the **Record Sort Expert** button.

---

b) In the **Record Sort Expert** dialog box, in the **Available Fields** list box, under **Employee**, select **Position** and add it to the **Sort Fields** list box.

c) In the **Sort Direction** section, verify that the **Ascending** option is selected.

d) Select **OK** to sort the data in ascending order.

e) Verify that the data in the **Position** field is sorted in ascending order.

| Position | Supervisor ID |
|---|---|
| Advertising Specialist | 13 |
| Business Manager | 2 |
| Inside Sales Coordinator | 5 |
| Mail Clerk | 10 |
| Marketing Associate | 13 |
| Marketing Director | 2 |
| Receptionist | 10 |
| Sales Manager | 2 |
| Sales Representative | 5 |
| Sales Representative | 5 |
| Sales Representative | 5 |
| Sales Representative | 5 |
| Sales Representative | 5 |
| Sales Representative | 5 |
| Vice President, Sales | |

3. View the SQL query created by Crystal Reports to request data.

a) Select **Database→Show SQL Query** to display the query.

b) In the **Show SQL Query** dialog box, observe the query.

c) Select **Close** to close the **Show SQL Query** dialog box.

d) Close the report without saving it.

4. Specify an SQL query to create a report that displays the supervisor ID and position sorted by the **Position** field.

 **Note:** When you write a query, use the grave accent key (`) which is situated to the left of the **1** key on the keyboard.

a) Select the **Blank report** link.

b) In the **Database Expert** dialog box, on the **Data** tab, in the **Available Data Sources** section, expand C:\095203Data\xtreme_B.mdb and double-click **Add Command**.

c) In the **Add Command To Report** dialog box, in the **Enter SQL query in the box below** text box, enter the following SQL query that will alphabetize the **Position** field from the **Employee** table:

```
SELECT Position, `Supervisor ID`
FROM Employee
ORDER BY Position
```

d) Select **OK**.

e) In the **Database Expert** dialog box, select **OK**.

f) In the **Field Explorer**, expand **Database Fields**, and then expand **Command**.

g) From the **Field Explorer**, drag the **Position** field to the 0-inch mark in the **Details** section.

h) Drag the **Supervisor ID** field to the 2-inch mark in the **Details** section.

i) Preview the report.

j) Verify that the data is alphabetized by the **Position** field, as specified in the SQL statement you entered.

5. Modify the query so that it lists each position only one time.

a) Select **Database→Database Expert**.

b) In the **Database Expert** dialog box, in the **Selected Tables** list box, right-click **Command** and select **Edit Command** to edit the query.

c) In the **Modify Command** dialog box, in the **Enter SQL query in the box below** text box, in the first
line, place the insertion point before the word "Position," type *DISTINCT* and press the **Spacebar**.

d) Compare your SQL statement with the following:

```
SELECT DISTINCT Position, `Supervisor ID`
FROM Employee
ORDER BY Position
```

e) Select **OK**.

f) In the **Database Expert** dialog box, select **OK**.

g) Verify that the repeating job names have been removed.

| Position | Supervisor ID |
|---|---|
| Advertising Specialist | 13 |
| Business Manager | 2 |
| Inside Sales Coordinator | 5 |
| Mail Clerk | 10 |
| Marketing Associate | 13 |
| Marketing Director | 2 |
| Receptionist | 10 |
| Sales Manager | 2 |
| Sales Representative | 5 |
| Vice President, Sales | |

h) Display the **Save As** dialog box.

i) Navigate to the **C:\095203Data\Using SQL Statement in Report Processing** folder.

j) Save the report as *My Sales Positions* and close it.

# TOPIC B

## Summarize Report Data

You created a report by writing an SQL query. There might be situations in which the retrieved data contains hundreds of records with redundant details.

Imagine having a report that contains several thousand records with redundant details. It may take several hours for you to comprehend the data and write complex programs to retrieve the desired results. By using SQL aggregate functions in a query, you can produce the desired summary result, thereby saving time.

## SQL Aggregate Functions

An *SQL aggregate function* is a function that produces a summary value for a group of values in a specified field. You can use aggregate functions in either the **SELECT** clause or the **HAVING** clause. Aggregates require an expression, which needs to be enclosed in parentheses.

 **Note:** SQL aggregate functions mostly require an added **GROUP BY** clause to find the total for each individual record, because the SQL aggregate functions return the value for only the records in a specified field.

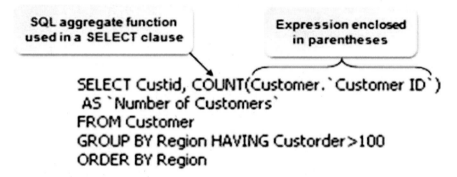

Figure 5-5: SQL aggregate functions.

### The Types of SQL Aggregate Functions

There are five types of SQL aggregate functions that you can use in an SQL query.

| Function | Description |
|----------|-------------|
| **AVG** | Calculates the average of values in a numeric field or expression. |
| **COUNT** | Determines the number of records that match the specified criteria. |
| **MAX** | Determines the greatest value in a specified field or expression. |
| **MIN** | Determines the smallest value in a specified field or expression. |
| **SUM** | Calculates the total of values in a numeric field or expression. |

 **Access the Checklist tile on your CHOICE Course screen for reference information and job aids on How to Summarize Report Data.**

# ACTIVITY 5-2
## Summarizing Report Data Using the COUNT Function

### Data File
C:\095203Data\xtreme_B.mdb

### Before You Begin
The Crystal Reports application is open.

### Scenario
You are working in the sales department of your organization, and you need to create a simple report counting the number of customers you have in each region.

---

1. Write an SQL statement that will return a count of all customers sorted by region.
   a) Select the **Blank report** link.
   b) In the **Database Expert** dialog box, in the **Available Data Sources** list box, expand **C:\095203Data \xtreme_B.mdb** and double-click **Add Command** to add a command to the report.
   c) In the **Add Command To Report** dialog box, in the **Enter SQL query in the box below** text box, create the following SQL statement that will return a count of all customers sorted by region:

   ```
   SELECT Region, COUNT (Customer.`Customer ID`) as `Number of Customers`
   FROM Customer
   GROUP BY Region
   ORDER BY Region
   ```
   d) Select **OK**.
   e) In the **Database Expert** dialog box, select **OK**.

2. Add fields from the query to the **Details** section of the report.
   a) In the **Field Explorer**, expand **Database Fields**, and then expand **Command**.
   b) Drag the **Region** field to the 0-inch mark in the **Details** section.
   c) Drag the **Number of Customers** field to the 2-inch mark in the **Details** section.
   d) Preview the report.
   e) Verify the summarized report data in the **Number of Customers** column.

   | Region | Number of Customers |
   | --- | --- |
   | Abu Dhabi | 1 |
   | AL | 3 |
   | Alsace | 2 |
   | Ankara | 1 |
   | Aquitaine | 2 |
   | AR | 1 |

   f) Save the report as *My Customer Count by Region*
   g) Close the report.

**Note:** To explore how to customize reports, access the Spotlight on **Publishing Reports Using DRS** presentation from the **Spotlight** tile on the CHOICE course screen.

# TOPIC C

## Create Joins Using SQL

You created reports and summarized data using SQL. When creating reports, you may need to retrieve data from two or more tables.

Creating a join using SQL enables you to create a report that includes fields from multiple tables. Therefore, all the data you need for your report is available.

## Joins

A *join* is a method of linking two or more tables together so that you can use data from the linked tables within a report. The **JOIN** keyword joins tables based on a common field. You can specify several types of joins within an SQL query.

Suppose you want to use fields from both the **Customer** and **Orders** tables within a single report, and you want to use an SQL query to generate the report. Both tables include a **Customer ID** field that you can use to join the tables. To include the **Customer Name** field from the **Customer** table, along with the **Order Date** and **Order Amount** fields from the **Orders** table, you can specify the following query.

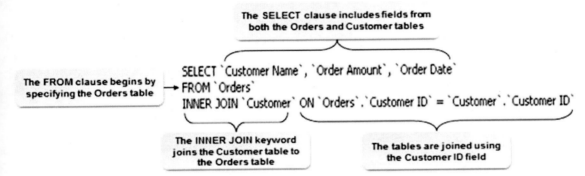

*Figure 5-6: An example of a statement linked with the JOIN keyword.*

### Joins by the WHERE Clause

At times, you may see joins specified within the **WHERE** clause, as in the following example:

```
SELECT Name, Amount
FROM Customer, Orders
WHERE Customer.ID = Orders.ID
```

This example would return the **Name** field from the **Customer** table and the **Amount** field from the **Orders** table. The two tables are joined by the **ID** field.

## Join Types

You can specify several types of joins within an SQL query.

| Join Type | Used To |
|---|---|
| Inner join | Access all the records in which the linked field value in both tables is an exact match.<br><br>Example:<br><br>`SELECT Name, Amount`<br>`FROM Orders`<br>`INNER JOIN Customer`<br>`ON Orders.ID = Customer.ID`<br><br>This query includes all records from each table whose **ID** field has a corresponding match in the other table. |
| Left outer join | Access all the records in which the linked field value in both tables matches, as well as all unmatched records from the table whose name directly follows the **FROM** keyword within the query, also known as the primary table.<br><br>Example:<br><br>`SELECT Name, Amount`<br>`FROM Orders`<br>`LEFT OUTER JOIN Customer`<br>`ON Orders.ID = Customer.ID`<br><br>This query includes all records from each table whose **ID** field has a corresponding match in the other table, along with all records from the **Orders** table. |
| Right outer join | Access all records in which the linked field value in both tables matches, as well as all unmatched records from the table whose name directly follows the **JOIN** keyword, also known as the lookup table.<br><br>Example:<br><br>`SELECT Name, Amount`<br>`FROM Orders`<br>`RIGHT OUTER JOIN Customer`<br>`ON Orders.ID = Customer.ID`<br><br>This query includes all records from each table whose **ID** field has a corresponding match in the other table, along with all records from the **Customer** table. |

 **Access the Checklist tile on your CHOICE Course screen for reference information and job aids on How to Create Joins Using SQL.**

# ACTIVITY 5-3
## Creating SQL Joins

### Data File
C:\095203Data\xtreme_B.mdb

### Before You Begin
The Crystal Reports application is open.

### Scenario
You need to create a report that lists the names of all employees in your organization, along with their country names. The employee name fields are available in the **Employee** table, but the country data is in the **Employee Addresses** table. Both of these tables have a common field named **Employee ID**. You need to retrieve the data based on the common field.

---

1. Display the **Add Command To Report** dialog box.
   a) Select the **Blank report** link.
   b) In the **Database Expert** dialog box, in the **Available Data Sources** list box, expand **C:\095203Data \xtreme_B.mdb** and double-click **Add Command** to display the **Add Command To Report** dialog box.

2. Write an SQL query that will retrieve the first and last names of employees, sorted by country.
   a) In the **Enter SQL query in the box below** text box, create the following query that uses the **Employee** table with inner-join data sorted by country:

   ```
   SELECT `First Name`, `Last Name`, `Country`
   FROM Employee
   INNER JOIN `Employee Addresses` ON Employee.`Employee ID`=`Employee
   Addresses`.`Employee ID`
   ORDER BY Country
   ```
   b) Select **OK**.
   c) In the **Database Expert** dialog box, select **OK**.

3. Add fields to the report.
   a) In the **Field Explorer**, expand **Database Fields**, and then expand **Command**.
   b) Drag the **First Name** field to the 0-inch mark in the **Details** section.
   c) Drag the **Last Name** field to the 1.5-inch mark in the **Details** section.
   d) Drag the **Country** field to the 4-inch mark in the **Details** section.
   e) Preview the report.

f) Verify that the employee names are displayed along with the country to which they belong.

| First Name | Last Name | Country |
|---|---|---|
| Caroline | Patterson | Canada |
| Tim | Smith | Canada |
| Albert | Hellstern | Canada |
| Laura | Callahan | Canada |
| Margaret | Peacock | Canada |
| Janet | Leverling | Canada |
| Andrew | Fuller | Canada |
| Nancy | Davolio | Canada |
| Laurent | Pereira | France |
| Xavier | Martin | France |
| Justin | Brid | France |
| Anne | Dodsworth | UK |
| Robert | King | UK |
| Michael | Suyama | UK |
| Steven | Buchanan | UK |

g) Save the report as *My Employees by Country*

h) Close the report.

# ACTIVITY 5-4
## Changing the Join Type

### Data Files

C:\095203Data\xtreme_B.mdb

C:\095203Data\Using SQL Statement in Report Processing\Productlist.rpt

### Before You Begin

The Crystal Reports application is open.

### Scenario

You have a report that contains the details of product names with their respective IDs; however, the report displays the names of all products ordered, regardless of whether the orders were paid. You want to modify the report so that it will generate all the existing product names along with their IDs for any paid orders. The report data is generated from two different tables, **Product** and **Purchases**. The product names are stored in the **Product** table and the details of purchases are stored in the **Purchases** table. Both tables are linked by a common field, **Product ID**.

1. View the existing SQL query.
   a) Open the **Productlist.rpt** file.
   b) Select **Database→Show SQL Query** to view the existing SQL query for the report.
   c) In the **Show SQL Query** dialog box, in the existing SQL query, verify that a left outer join exists based on the **Product ID** field. The report displays all records from each table that have a matching **Product ID**.
   d) Select **Close**.
   e) Preview the report and note the number of records returned.

2. Modify the join type so the report includes only records for products that have paid purchases.
   a) On the **Experts** toolbar, select the **Database Expert** button.
   b) In the **Database Expert** dialog box, on the **Data** tab, in the **Selected Tables** list box, under **C:\095203Data\xtreme_B.mdb**, right-click **Command** and select **Edit Command** to modify the existing SQL query.
   c) In the **Modify Command** dialog box, in the **Enter SQL query in the box below** text box, click in a blank area to deselect the code.
   d) In the third line of the code, replace the words "LEFT OUTER JOIN" by typing *INNER JOIN* to change the join type from a left outer join to an inner join.
   e) Select **OK** to execute the updated SQL query.
   f) In the **Database Expert** dialog box, select **OK**.
   g) Preview the report and note that fewer records were returned than the last time. You are now seeing only the products that have paid purchases.
   h) Save the file as *My Productlist*
   i) Close the report.

# TOPIC D

## Create Subqueries

You retrieved data using one SQL query; however, there may be occasions when using one SQL query doesn't fulfill your reporting needs.

You may need to extract more complex data, which may not be possible through simple querying methods. For example, you may want to create a report that includes an aggregate function to display the total count of orders, along with the **Order Date** and **Order Amount** fields. Using simple **SELECT** clause structures won't produce the fields you want. Instead, a subquery would allow you to generate the desired report data.

### Subqueries

A *subquery* is a secondary **SELECT** clause that is nested inside an outer query. It can be used within a **SELECT**, **FROM**, **WHERE**, or **HAVING** clause and must be enclosed in parentheses. In SQL statements that contain a subquery, the condition inside the subquery is evaluated first and the condition of the outer query is evaluated next. A subquery can contain multiple inner queries, each of which is enclosed in parentheses.

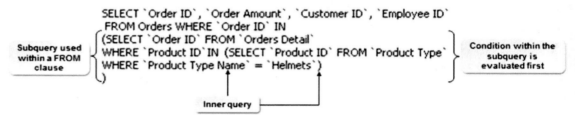

*Figure 5–7: A subquery used within a clause.*

### The Performance Information Dialog Box

You can use the **Performance Information** dialog box to assess the performance of a report. It contains many nodes that enable you to view statistics about the various aspects of the report that are critical to its performance.

| Node | Enables You To |
|------|----------------|
| **Report Definition** | View the various types of content in your report, such as the number of database fields, summary fields, and file-format schema. |
| **Saved Data** | View report details, such as the number of records and data sources in a report, or the size of saved records and memo fields. |
| **Processing** | View details of the factors that determine the processing of your report data, such as grouping, sorting, or record selection done on the database server. |
| **Latest Report Changes** | View the latest changes made to the report. |

| Node | Enables You To |
|------|----------------|
| **Performance Timing** | View statistical details regarding your report performance, such as the time taken to open a report or format the pages. |

 **Access the Checklist tile on your CHOICE Course screen for reference information and job aids on How to Create Subqueries.**

# ACTIVITY 5–5
## Creating Subqueries

### Data Files

C:\095203Data\xtreme_B.mdb

C:\095203Data\Using SQL Statement in Report Processing\Latest Orders.rpt

### Before You Begin

The Crystal Reports application is open.

### Scenario

You have a report that lists the most recent order date for each customer. You want to ensure the database server is processing the report data and sending only the necessary data to your computer.

1. View the existing SQL query.
   a) Open the **Latest Orders.rpt** file.
   b) Select **Report→Select Expert→Group**.
   c) In the **Select Expert -- Group** dialog box, on the **Max of Orders.Order Date** tab, verify that the following formula is listed, which limits the records based on an aggregate calculation on the **Customer Name** group:

      ```
      {Orders.Order Date}=Maximum ({Orders.Order Date},
      {Customer.Customer.Name})
      ```
   d) In the **Select Expert -- Group** dialog box, select **OK**.
   e) Select **Database→Show SQL Query**.
   f) In the **Show SQL Query** dialog box, verify that Crystal Reports has processed the SQL query to limit the records based on the formula you viewed in the **Select Expert** dialog box.
   g) Select **Close**.

2. View the performance information for the report.
   a) Select **Report→Performance Information** to view the report performance.
   b) In the **Performance Information** dialog box, under **Latest Orders.rpt**, select **Saved Data**.
   c) Verify that the total number of records is **2164** and all the records are selected by the existing SQL query.
   d) Select **Processing** to view the processing speed.
   e) Verify that the number of summary values is **266**.
   f) Select **Performance Timing** to view the time taken by the report to open and format pages.

    | **Note:** The values for the performance timing of a report may vary from one system to another depending on the system settings and performance.

   g) Select **Close**.
   h) Close the report without saving it.

3. Create a report that generates the same output but uses an SQL query that specifies processing will occur on the remote server.
   a) Select the **Blank report** link.
   b) In the **Database Expert** dialog box, in the **Available Data Sources** list box, under **My Connections**, expand **C:\095203Data\xtreme_B.mdb** and double-click **Add Command**.

c) In the **Add Command To Report** dialog box, in the **Enter SQL query in the box below** text box, create the following SQL query to specify processing occurs on the remote server:

```
SELECT `Customer Name`,
(SELECT Max(`Order Date`)
FROM Orders
WHERE Orders.`Customer ID`=Customer.`Customer ID`)
AS LastOrder
FROM Customer
ORDER BY `Customer Name`
```

d) Select **OK**.

e) In the **Database Expert** dialog box, select **OK**.

4. Add fields to the report.

a) In the **Field Explorer**, expand **Database Fields**, and then expand **Command**.

b) From the **Field Explorer**, drag the **Customer Name** field to the 0-inch mark in the **Details** section.

c) Drag the **LastOrder** field to the 2-inch mark in the **Details** section.

d) Preview the report.

e) Verify that the report displays data for the **Customer Name** and **LastOrder** fields.

f) Right-click the first date under **LastOrder** and select **Format Field**.

g) On the **Format Editor**, on the **Date and Time** tab, select the **03/01/1999** format.

h) Select **OK**.

5. View the performance information for the current report.

a) Select **Report→Performance Information**.

b) Select **Saved Data**.

c) Verify that the total number of records selected is only **267** compared to **2164** in the earlier report. This indicates the database server has processed the query and returned only the data specified by the condition in the subquery.

d) Select **Processing** to find the processing speed of the report.

e) Verify that the number of summary values is zero compared to the **266** summary values retrieved earlier.

f) Select **Performance Timing** to find the time taken by the report to load.

g) Verify that the time taken for the report to open is zero milliseconds (ms).

h) Select **Close**.

i) Save the report as *My Latest Orders*

j) Close the report.

 **Note:** To explore how to customize reports, access the Spotlight on **Improving Report Performance** presentation from the **Spotlight** tile on the CHOICE course screen.

# TOPIC E

## Create an SQL Expression Field

You created subqueries to return a set of data on which a report can be based. However, there may be times when you only care about the resulting value of a formula, not the fields used in calculating the value.

You know that functions within formulas must be processed by Crystal Reports. You can replace the function in a Crystal Reports record selection formula with an equivalent SQL expression field, thereby pushing record processing to the database server. This makes your report processing faster and more efficient.

### SQL Expression Fields

An *SQL expression field* is a formula written in SQL that usually results in a calculated field that a report can use. SQL expressions are more commonly used than equivalent Crystal Reports formulas, because formulas are processed on the database server. SQL expression fields are created using the **SQL Expression Editor** in the **Formula Workshop** window. Each expression field contains a function followed by the specified database field enclosed in parentheses.

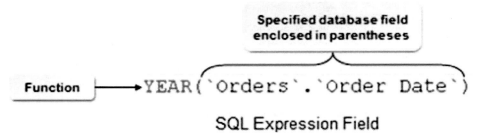

*Figure 5-8: An instance of an SQL expression field.*

 **Access the Checklist tile on your CHOICE Course screen for reference information and job aids on How to Create an SQL Expression Field.**

# ACTIVITY 5–6
## Creating an SQL Expression Field

### Data Files

C:\095203Data\xtreme_B.mdb

C:\095203Data\Using SQL Statement in Report Processing\2015 Canada Sales.rpt

### Before You Begin

The Crystal Reports application is open.

### Scenario

The **2015 Canada Sales.rpt** report summarizes the 2015 sales. Although the report runs well for now, you anticipate that as the amount of data displayed by the report increases, it will take several minutes to run. You want to speed up the processing of this report.

1. View the selection formula.
   a) Open the **2015 Canada Sales.rpt** file.
   b) Select **Report→Select Expert→Record**.
   c) In the **Select Expert -- Record** dialog box, verify that the following formula is listed:
   ```
   {Customer.Country}in["Canada"]and
   Year({Orders.Order Date})=2015
   ```
   d) Select **OK**.

2. View the existing SQL query.
   a) Select **Database→Show SQL Query**.
   b) Verify that the following SQL query is listed in the **Show SQL Query** dialog box:
   ```
   SELECT `Customer`.`Customer Name`, `Customer`.`Customer ID`,
   `Orders_Detail`.`Quantity`,`Product`.`Product Name`,
   `Orders`.`Order Date`, `Customer`.`Country`
   FROM ((`Customer` `Customer` LEFT OUTER JOIN `Orders` `Orders` ON
   `Customer`.`Customer ID`=`Orders`.`Customer ID`) LEFT OUTER JOIN
   `Orders Detail` `Orders_Detail` ON `Orders`.`Order
   ID`=`Orders_Detail`.`Order ID`) LEFT OUTER JOIN `Product` `Product` ON
   `Orders_Detail`.`Product ID`=`Product`.`Product ID`
   WHERE `Customer`.`Country`='Canada'
   ```
   c) Select **Close**.

3. Build an SQL expression.
   a) In the **Field Explorer**, select **SQL Expression Fields**, and then select the **New** button to create a new SQL formula.
   b) In the **SQL Expression Name** dialog box, in the **Name** text box, type *YearFilter* and then select **OK**.
   c) In the **Formula Workshop - SQL Expression Editor - YearFilter** window, in the **Function Tree**, expand **Date/Time**.
   d) Scroll down and double-click **YEAR()**.
   e) In the **Field Tree**, expand the **Orders** table and double-click **Order Date** to filter the year data based on the order date.
   f) Compare your formula with the following:
   ```
   YEAR(`Orders`.`Order Date`)
   ```

g) Check the formula for errors, and then select **Save and close**.

4. Delete the existing non-SQL selection formula in the report.
   a) Select **Report→Select Expert→Record**.
   b) In the **Select Expert -- Record** dialog box, select the **Orders.Order Date** tab.
   c) Select **Delete** to delete the tab and remove that part of the existing formula. The **Customer.Country** tab and formula will remain.

5. Replace the SQL expression with a new formula and refresh the records.
   a) In the **Select Expert -- Record** dialog box, select the **<New>** tab.
   b) In the **Choose Field** dialog box, under **Report Fields**, select **YearFilter**, and then select **OK**.
   c) Verify that a new tab titled **%YearFilter** is displayed.
   d) On the **%YearFilter** tab, from the drop-down list, select **is equal to**.
   e) In the text box located to the right of the drop-down list, type *2015* as the criterion for the filter formula.
   f) Select **OK**.
   g) In the **Change In Record Selection Formula** dialog box, select **Refresh Data**.
   h) Verify that the same records are returned.

6. View the SQL query to examine the **WHERE** clause.
   a) Select **Database→Show SQL Query**.
   b) Verify that the **WHERE** clause is in the new formula.
   c) In the **Show SQL Query** dialog box, select **Close**.

7. Save and close the report.
   a) Save the report as *My 2015 Canada Sales*
   b) Close the report.

# Summary

In this lesson, you enhanced report processing by writing SQL statements. The ability to incorporate SQL into reports will allow you and others to access report data quickly and efficiently, and perform reporting functions that aren't possible otherwise.

**What clause function will you use to extract data from a database?**

**List a few examples of reports that inhibit server-side processing.**

 **Note:** To explore how to customize reports, access the Spotlight on **Including Flash Files in Reports** presentation from the **Spotlight** tile on the CHOICE course screen.

 **Note:** Check your CHOICE Course screen for opportunities to interact with your classmates, peers, and the larger CHOICE online community about the topics covered in this course or other topics you are interested in. From the Course screen you can also access available resources for a more continuous learning experience.

# 6 | Creating Complex Formulas

Lesson Time: 55 minutes

## Lesson Objectives

In this lesson, you will:

- Work with loops.

- Work with arrays.

## Lesson Introduction

You have created reports and worked with simple formulas. Now you want to perform complex calculations on report data.

You want to create a sales report that involves complex calculations being performed on data. However, the built-in functions available in SAP® Crystal Reports® alone may not give you the desired output. Fortunately, Crystal Reports allows you to create complex formulas that are beneficial when presenting voluminous data as reports.

# TOPIC A

## Work with Loops

You created reports using basic formulas. Now you may want to use complex formulas and execute a set of commands on data when a given condition is satisfied.

You need to perform a calculation that requires a particular group of commands to be executed repeatedly for a specific number of times. You aren't sure of the number of times the set of commands needs to be repeated, nor do you have the time to write the set of statements as many times as you would like them to execute. By creating loops, you will be able to execute a set of commands repeatedly until the given condition is satisfied.

## Loops

A *loop* is a programming logic that allows you to repeatedly execute a set of statements contained within it, saving you from having to write a block of code over and over again. Each repetition is called an iteration. A loop checks for a condition and, when it's met, the statements within the loop are executed. When a loop contains one or more loops within it, it's called a nested loop.

### Loops in Crystal Reports

Crystal Reports provides three categories of loops: condition tested loops, counted loops, and indefinite loops. Condition tested loops repeatedly execute a set of programming statements until a condition is met. Counted loops repeatedly execute a set of programming statements for a specified number of iterations. Indefinite loops repeatedly execute a set of programming statements indefinitely. An indefinite loop is exited only when the computer is turned off or crashes. Indefinite loops are not supported in Crystal Reports. The application displays an error message when encountering an indefinite loop. A Crystal Reports formula can have one or more loops with a maximum of 100,000 iterations only. You can use the **Do**, **For**, and **While** loops in a Crystal Reports formula.

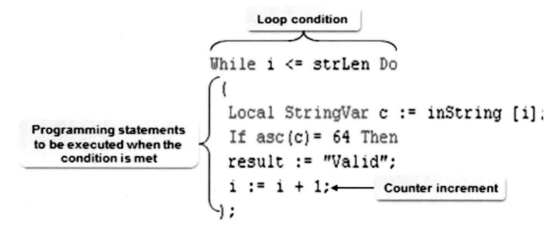

*Figure 6–1: Loop example.*

 **Access the Checklist tile on your CHOICE Course screen for reference information and job aids on How to Work with Loops.**

# ACTIVITY 6-1
## Working with Loops

### Data Files

C:\095203Data\xtreme_B.mdb

C:\095203Data\Creating Complex Formula\Customer Mails.rpt

### Before You Begin

The Crystal Reports application is open.

### Scenario

You are the owner of a shopping mall and have a lot of customers. You decide to send them seasonal greetings and information about the various offers in order to boost sales. You have a list of your customers' contact email IDs and decide to validate them so your mail server is not clogged with error messages of invalid email IDs.

1. Create a formula for validating email IDs.
    a) Display the **Open** dialog box.
    b) Navigate to the **C:\095203Data\Creating Complex Formula** folder.
    c) Select **Customer Mails.rpt**, and then select **Open**.
    d) In the **Field Explorer**, select **Formula Fields**, and then select the **New** button.
    e) In the **Formula Name** dialog box, in the **Name** text box, type *Validate* and then select **OK**.
    f) In the **Formula Workshop - Formula Editor - Validate** window, in the **Definition** area, enter the following code to validate the email IDs:

```
Local StringVar inString;
Local NumberVar strLen;
Local stringVar result := "InValid";
Local numberVar i := 1;
inString :={Customer.E-mail};
strLen :=length(instring);
While i <= strLen Do
(
Local stringVar c := instring [i];
If asc(c)= 64 Then
result := "Valid";
i := i + 1;
);
result
```

    g) Check the formula for errors, and then select **Save and close**.

2. Add fields to the report.
    a) In the **Design** view, in the **Field Explorer**, expand **Database Fields**, and then expand **Customer**.
    b) Drag the **Customer Name** field to the 0-inch mark in the **Details** section.
    c) Drag the **E-mail** field to the 2-inch mark in the **Details** section.
    d) In the **Field Explorer**, under **Formula Fields**, drag the **Validate** field to the 4-inch mark in the **Details** section.

3. Preview and save the report.

a) Preview the report.
b) Verify that the email IDs are showing as valid.
c) Save the report as *My Customer Mails* and close it.

# TOPIC B

# Work with Arrays

You created loops and obtained multiple values of the same data type as output. You may now want to store and work with multiple values of the same data type.

You have to create a report in which you make calculations on multiple values of the same data type. Declaring a variable for each value may not be feasible. However, by working with arrays, you will be able to store all values using only one variable and perform the calculations.

## Arrays

An *array* is a data structure that contains a large amount of data of the same type. Each individual data item in an array is referred to as an array element. Arrays are numbered uniquely starting with a zero. This numeral is called an array index. The memory size of the array depends on the type of data to be stored. Arrays are of two types: static arrays and dynamic arrays. An array in which the size of the array is defined during array declaration is called a static array. An array in which no size is defined during array declaration is called a dynamic array.

 **Access the Checklist tile on your CHOICE Course screen for reference information and job aids on How to Work with Arrays.**

# ACTIVITY 6–2
## Working with Arrays

### Data Files

C:\095203Data\xtreme_B.mdb

C:\095203Data\Creating Complex Formula\Running Total Array.rpt

### Before You Begin

The Crystal Reports application is open.

### Scenario

You have a sales report and want to create a running total for the sales value. However, you don't want to use a running total field. Instead, you want to use formulas in order to obtain the running total.

---

1.  Group the report by the **Order ID** field.
    a)  Open the **Running Total Array.rpt** report.
    b)  On the **Insert** toolbar, select the **Insert Group** button.
    c)  In the **Insert Group** dialog box, on the **Common** tab, from the first drop-down list, select **Orders.Order ID**, and then select **OK**.

2.  Create a formula that will use an array to calculate the running total.
    a)  Create the following formula called *Running Total* that uses an array to calculate the running total:

    ```
    WhilePrintingRecords;
    currencyVar Array Runtot;
    numberVar n;
    n := n + 1;
    Redim Preserve Runtot[n];
    Runtot[n] := Sum ({Orders.Order Amount}, {Orders.Order ID});
    Sum (Runtot[1 to n])
    ```

    b)  Check the formula for errors, and then select **Save and close**.

3.  Add the running total formula field to the report.
    a)  Switch to the **Design** view.
    b)  From the **Field Explorer**, drag the **Running Total** formula to the 6.5-inch mark in the **Details** section.
    c)  In the **RHb** section, right-click and select **Suppress (No Drill-Down)**.
    d)  In the **GH1** section, right-click and select **Suppress (No Drill-Down)**.
    e)  In the **GF1** section, right-click and select **Suppress (No Drill-Down)**.

4.  Align the fields.
    a)  In the **PH** section, select the **Running Total** field heading and press the **Up Arrow**.
    b)  In the **PH** section, right-click and select **Arrange Lines**.
    c)  Preview the report.
    d)  View the running totals.
    e)  Save the report as *My Running Total Array* and close it.

---

# Summary

In this lesson, you created complex formulas. By performing complex calculations required to present data, you obtained the desired results.

**In what situations would you use a loop or an array to perform complex calculations?**

**What type of loop would you use the most often?**

 **Note:** Check your CHOICE Course screen for opportunities to interact with your classmates, peers, and the larger CHOICE online community about the topics covered in this course or other topics you are interested in. From the Course screen you can also access available resources for a more continuous learning experience.

# 7 | Adding Charts to Reports

**Lesson Time: 1 hour, 30 minutes**

## Lesson Objectives

In this lesson, you will:

- Create charts.

- Create a chart with drill-down.

- Create a top N chart.

- Create a cross-tab chart.

- Create charts for grouped data.

- Format a chart.

- Create a chart template.

## Lesson Introduction

You used SQL queries to process report data. Now you may want to represent report data graphically.

You have to present sales data as a large report at a meeting. However, the audience may find it difficult to comprehend multiple pages of textual content. By adding charts to your reports, you will be able to present data graphically, making the data easier to understand.

# TOPIC A

## Create Charts

You used SQL queries to present data in a report. Now you want to present data in the form of charts.

Suppose you have a report that contains information that is displayed in columns and rows. By creating charts, you will be able to identify trends easily using the data points provided to measure or compare data.

### Charts

A *chart* is a type of graphic used to present tabular data graphically. To create a chart, you need at least one numeric field or text field with aggregate functions. Charts are of different types and they can be easily changed from one type to another.

Figure 7-1: A sample chart.

### Chart Types

When you create a chart in SAP® Crystal Reports®, it's important that you select the type of chart that best matches the data to be shown.

| Type | Displays |
|------|----------|
| **Bar** | Data using bars side by side. It's best suited for comparing group values. |
| **Line** | Trends in data as a series of points connected by a line. It's best suited for displaying data for many groups. |
| **Area** | Data as areas that are filled with color or patterns. It's best suited for displaying data for a limited number of groups. |
| **Pie** | Data as percentages in a pie, split and filled with color or patterns. It's normally used for one group of data. |
| **Doughnut** | Data as sections of a circle or doughnut, similar to a pie chart. It can display the grand total in the hole in the middle. |

| Type | Displays |
|------|----------|
| **3D Riser** | The extremes in data in a series of three-dimensional objects, side by side, in a three-dimensional plane. This chart type is similar to a bar chart. |
| **3D Surface** | A topographic view of multiple sets of data. |
| **XY Scatter** | A group of plotted points that represent specific data in a pool of information, allowing the user to determine trends. |
| **Radar** | A group of data at the perimeter of the radar and numeric values from the center of the radar to the perimeter, allowing the user to determine how specific group data relates to the whole group data. |
| **Bubble** | Data as a series of bubbles. It's similar to an XY scatter chart. |
| **Stock** | High and low values for data. It's useful for monitoring financial or sales activities. |
| **Numeric Axis** | A bar, line, or area chart that uses a numeric or date/time field as its **On Change Of** field. |
| **Gauge** | Values graphically as points on a gauge. It's usually used for one group of data. |
| **Gantt** | A horizontal bar chart that provides a graphical illustration of a schedule. The horizontal axis displays a time span. The vertical axis displays a series of tasks or events. |
| **Funnel** | Data as percentages that add up to 100 percent, but it uses a funnel shape to display data percentages. It's often used for pipeline analysis for sales forecasts. It's similar to a pie chart or a stacked bar chart. |
| **Histogram** | The frequency with which data occurs. It's a type of bar chart. |

## Chart Layouts

Depending on what data you need to display, you can select one of four chart layouts.

| Layout | Used To |
|--------|---------|
| **Advanced** | Graph multiple chart values when there are no group or summary fields in a report. You can't use this layout if the chart has been placed in the **Details** section. |
| **Group** | Graph data in summary fields. For this layout, you must place the chart in a summary section, such as a **Report Header**, **Report Footer**, **Group Header**, or **Group Footer**. |
| **Cross-Tab** | Graph data in an existing cross-tab object, which is a grid that includes rows, columns, and summary fields. |
| **OLAP** | Graph data in an existing OLAP grid, which is used to display OLAP data. OLAP grid objects look and act much like cross-tab objects, but they are designed specifically for OLAP data. |

## Chart Elements

A chart has numerous elements that each have a specific function.

| Chart Element | Function |
|---|---|
| Axis | Indicates the line that borders one side of the plot area in a chart, providing a reference for measuring or comparing data. The Y axis is usually vertical; the X axis is usually horizontal. |
| Data points | Represents the individual values in a chart. |
| Marker | Indicates a bar, area, plot, slice, or symbol that represents a data series in a chart. |
| Data series | Indicates the related data points plotted collectively in a chart, represented by a marker. |
| Axes labels | Contains text that provides additional information about a marker in relation to the axis scale. |
| Legend | Indicates a box that identifies the patterns or colors assigned to a data series. |
| Plot area | Indicates an area within the axes of a chart that includes the data series. |

## The Chart Expert Dialog Box

You can use the **Chart Expert** dialog box to specify the settings for a chart. This dialog box consists of six tabs.

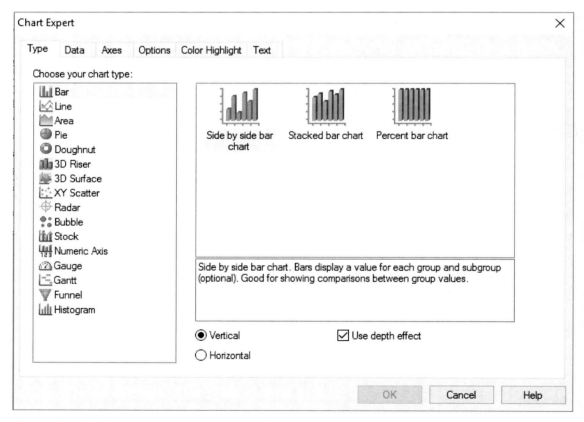

*Figure 7–2: The Type tab displayed in the Chart Expert dialog box.*

The following table provides a description of each of the tabs available in the **Chart Expert** dialog box.

| Tab | Used To |
| --- | --- |
| **Type** | Specify the type of chart to be displayed. It's also used to specify depth-effect settings. |
| **Data** | Specify the layout and fields to be used for the chart. |
| **Axes** | Specify the settings for chart axes. It's not displayed for the pie, doughnut, Gantt, or funnel chart. |
| **Options** | Specify the settings for chart color, data points, legends, and markers. The options on the tab vary according to the chart type selected. |
| **Color Highlight** | Specify the condition on which colors are to be applied to the values in the chart. |
| **Text** | Specify the titles, footnotes, and axis titles for the chart. |

 **Access the Checklist tile on your CHOICE Course screen for reference information and job aids on How to Create Charts.**

# ACTIVITY 7–1
## Creating a Bar Chart

### Data Files

C:\095203Data\xtreme_B.mdb

C:\095203Data\Adding Charts to Reports\Glove Helmet Sales.rpt

### Before You Begin

The Crystal Reports application is open.

### Scenario

You're getting ready to present the glove and helmet sales figures for the European division at the company's weekly sales meeting. The printed report doesn't represent the data adequately and it isn't easy to identify the trends in sales. In order to ensure that the presentation is easy to comprehend, you want to represent the data graphically in the form of a bar diagram with each value indicated along with its name.

1. Create a bar chart to show total helmets sold by country.
   a) Select **Open File** to display the **Open** dialog box.
   b) Navigate to the **C:\095203Data\Adding Charts to Reports** folder.
   c) Select **Glove Helmet Sales.rpt**, and then select **Open**.

   d) Switch to the **Design** view, and on the **Insert** toolbar, select the **Insert Chart** button.
   e) At the top-left margin of the **RH** section, click to place the chart.
   f) Right-click the chart and select **Chart Expert**.
   g) In the **Chart Expert** dialog box, on the **Type** tab, in the **Choose your chart type** section, verify that **Bar** is selected.
   h) Select the **Data** tab.
   i) On the **Data** tab, in the **Layout** section, verify that **Group** is selected.
   j) In the **Data** section, verify that **Customer.Country** is selected in the **On change of** drop-down list and **Sum of @Helmets** is selected in the **Show** drop-down list.

2. Change the bar size and display values on each of the bars.
   a) On the **Options** tab, in the **Data points** section, check the **Show value** check box.
   b) In the **Customize settings** section, from the **Bar size** drop-down list, select **Average**.

3. Change the chart and data titles.
   a) On the **Text** tab, in the **Titles** section, uncheck the **Auto-Text** check box corresponding to the **Title** text box, select the default text, and type *Helmets Sold Per Country*
   b) Uncheck the **Auto-Text** check box corresponding to the **Data title** text box, select the default text, and type *Helmets*
   c) Select **OK**.
   d) Preview the report.
   e) Save the report as *My Glove Helmet Sales* and close it.

# TOPIC B

## Create a Chart with Drill-Down

You created charts. Now you want to create a chart for summary data and display the detailed information only on demand.

When you present information from reports that contain drill-down data, the audience may find it too difficult to comprehend the drill-down data if it's represented in rows and columns. By creating a chart with drill-down, you can enhance user comprehension and the report's visual appeal.

 **Access the Checklist tile on your CHOICE Course screen for reference information and job aids on How to Create a Chart with Drill-Down.**

# ACTIVITY 7-2
## Creating a Pie Chart with Drill-Down

### Data Files
C:\095203Data\xtreme_B.mdb

C:\095203Data\Adding Charts to Reports\Helmet Sales by Type.rpt

### Before You Begin
The Crystal Reports application is open.

### Scenario
You have a report named Helmet Sales by Type that displays helmet sales for a select group of customers. It's a simple report; however, the information may be difficult to interpret. You need to create a pie chart to represent the information graphically so users can easily analyze the data.

1.  Create a pie chart to display the quantity data based on the product color.
    a)  Open the **Helmet Sales by Type.rpt** report.
    b)  In the **Design** view, on the **Insert** toolbar, select the **Insert Chart** button.
    c)  In the upper-left corner of the **RH** section, click to place the chart, which automatically opens the **Chart Expert** dialog box.
    d)  In the **Chart Expert** dialog box, on the **Type** tab, in the **Choose your chart type** list box, select **Pie**.
    e)  On the **Data** tab, in the **Layout** section, select **Group**.
    f)  In the **On change of** drop-down list, verify that **Product.Size** is selected.
    g)  In the **Show** drop-down list, verify that **Sum of Orders_Detail.Quantity** is selected.
    h)  Select **OK**.

2.  Preview the report.
    a)  Preview the report and verify the chart correctly displays the quantity by size.
    b)  Place the mouse pointer over the slice labeled **sm**, and verify that the mouse pointer changes to a magnifying glass, indicating the chart is a drill-down.

    A tooltip also displays the underlying details for that slice of the pie.
    c)  Double-click the slice and scroll down.
    d)  Verify that details for the slice are displayed below the pie chart.
    e)  Save the report as *My Helmet Sales by Type*
    f)  Close the report.

# TOPIC C

# Create a Top N Chart

You created a chart with drill-down. At times, it may be important that you display only a portion of data, such as the top-three values in a report.

You have a sales report that is created based on the sales per region. You want to create a chart that will display the top-three sellers in a given category while ignoring all other sellers. By creating a top N chart, you will be able to display data that falls within a specified ranking criterion.

## Top N Charts

A *top N chart* is a type of chart that allows you to narrow down data results by specifying the rank criteria in the **Group Sort Expert** dialog box. "N" represents the number of values to be displayed for the results. A report must contain a summary value in order for you to perform the top N selection. The top N value must be between 1 and 32,766 for groups, and between 0 and 100 for percentages. The report data that doesn't meet the top N criteria can either be displayed in a single group or eliminated from the report.

 **Access the Checklist tile on your CHOICE Course screen for reference information and job aids on How to Create a Top N Chart.**

# ACTIVITY 7–3
## Creating a Top N Chart

### Data Files

C:\095203Data\xtreme_B.mdb

C:\095203Data\Adding Charts to Reports\Sales by Country.rpt

### Before You Begin

The Crystal Reports application is open.

### Scenario

You have a bar chart that displays sales of helmets in five countries: Australia, Canada, England, Germany, and USA. You want to view the top-three regions within each country. You also want to display the data as currency.

---

1. Place a copy of the chart titled **Last Year's Sales By Country** in the group footer.
   a) Open the **Sales by Country.rpt** report.
   b) In the **Design** view, in the **RH** section, right-click the chart and select **Copy**.
   c) In a blank area of the report, right-click and select **Paste**.
   d) At the top-left corner of the **GF1** section, click to place the chart.

2. Replace the **Country** field with the **Region** field for sorting.
   a) In the **GF1** section, right-click the chart and select **Chart Expert**.
   b) In the **Chart Expert** dialog box, on the **Data** tab, in the **On change of** list box, remove the **Customer.Country - A** field by selecting the field and then selecting the left-arrow button.
   c) In the **Available Fields** list box, under **Customer**, scroll down and add the **Region** field to the **On change of** list box.

3. Display the top-three customers in each region.
   a) In the **On change of** list box, select **Customer.Region - A**, and then select **TopN**.
   b) In the **Group Sort Expert** dialog box, on the **Customer.Region** tab, from the **For this group sort** drop-down list, select **Top N**.
   c) Verify that in the **based on** drop-down list, **Sum of Customer.Last Year's Sales** is selected.
   d) In the **Where N is** text box, double-click and type *3*
   e) Verify that the **Include Others, with the name** check box is unchecked, and then select **OK**.

4. Change the format for the data points.
   a) On the **Options** tab, in the **Data points** section, check the **Show value** check box.
   b) From the **Number format** drop-down list, select **$1.00**.

5. Change the chart title to **Top-Three Regions**.
   a) On the **Text** tab, in the **Titles** section, uncheck the **Auto-Text** check box corresponding to the **Title** text box, select the default text, and type *Top-Three Regions*
   b) Select **OK**.
   c) Preview the report.
   d) Verify that the chart displays the top-three regions in each country.
   e) Save the report as *My Sales by Country* and close it.

---

# TOPIC D

## Create a Cross-Tab Chart

You created a top N chart based on a single data field. You may now want to create a chart based on multiple data fields.

There may be situations in which you need to present data based on multiple fields. By creating cross-tab charts, you will be able to represent data in multiple fields graphically so the values are easy to comprehend.

## Cross-Tab Charts

A *cross-tab chart* is a chart that displays summary information graphically from a cross-tab report. A cross-tab must be present in the report in order for you to insert a cross-tab chart. You can subdivide the data being displayed in the chart by using the secondary row or column field.

 **Access the Checklist tile on your CHOICE Course screen for reference information and job aids on How to Create a Cross-Tab Chart.**

# ACTIVITY 7–4
## Creating a Cross–Tab Chart

### Data Files

C:\095203Data\xtreme_B.mdb

C:\095203Data\Adding Charts to Reports\Bike Sales.rpt

### Before You Begin

The Crystal Reports application is open.

### Scenario

You have a cross-tab report that displays the 2014–2016 sales of bikes by product name. You want to summarize the data by product type with totals and percentages for comparison.

1. Insert cross-tab data charts to display a chart for each product name and to segregate the data in a chart by employee name.
   a) Open the **Bike Sales.rpt** report.
   b) In the **Design** view, on the **Insert** toolbar, select the **Insert Chart** button.
   c) At the top-left corner of the **RF** section, click to place the chart and automatically open the **Chart Expert** dialog box.
   d) In the **Chart Expert** dialog box, on the **Data** tab, in the **Layout** section, select **Cross-Tab**.
   e) Verify that in the **On change of** drop-down list, **Product.Product Name** is selected.
   f) From the **Subdivided by** drop-down list, select **Employee.First Name**.

2. Change the chart type to display data using multiple 3D pie charts of average pie size.
   a) On the **Type** tab, in the **Choose your chart type** list box, select **Pie**.
   b) In the right pane, select **Multiple pie chart**.
   c) Check the **Use depth effect** check box.
   d) On the **Options** tab, in the **Data points** section, uncheck the **Show label** check box.
   e) In the **Customize settings** section, from the **Pie size** drop-down list, select **Average**.

3. Change the title of the chart.
   a) On the **Text** tab, in the **Titles** section, uncheck the **Auto-Text** check box corresponding to the **Title** text box.
   b) In the **Title** text box, replace the default text by typing *Summary by Product Name & Employee Name*
   c) Select **OK**.

4. Preview the chart.
   a) Preview the report.
   b) Save the report as *My Bike Sales* and close it.

# TOPIC E

## Create Charts for Grouped Data

You have created cross-tab charts. Now you want to display report data that has to be grouped based on a criterion. The data would be represented better graphically.

You have to create a customer sales report with data grouped based on the order date. The report would run for pages, so it would be tedious to present during a meeting. By creating a chart for grouped data, you will be able to assess the data for each grouping graphically.

 **Access the Checklist tile on your CHOICE Course screen for reference information and job aids on How to Create Charts for Grouped Data.**

# ACTIVITY 7-5
## Presenting a Chart by Group

### Data Files

C:\095203Data\xtreme_B.mdb

C:\095203Data\Adding Charts to Reports\Total Helmet Sales.rpt

### Before You Begin

The Crystal Reports application is open.

### Scenario

The Total Helmet Sales report contains a pie chart that summarizes the total helmet sales for four customers. You need to add a chart to each group that displays the percentage of helmet sales by helmet type for each customer.

---

1. Preview the existing chart and include a new 3D pie chart in the **GF1** section.
   a) Open the **Total Helmet Sales.rpt** file and preview the report.
   b) Verify that the chart displays the percentage of helmet sales by helmet type for all customers.
   c) Switch to the **Design** view.
   d) On the **Insert** toolbar, select the **Insert Chart** button.
   e) Click at the top-left corner of the **GF1** section to place the chart and automatically open the **Chart Expert** dialog box.
   f) In the **Chart Expert** dialog box, on the **Type** tab, in the **Choose your chart type** list box, select **Pie**.
   g) Check the **Use depth effect** check box to make the pie three-dimensional.

2. Base the pie chart on the product name so it displays the quantity of each product ordered by customer.
   a) Select the **Data** tab.
   b) In the **Data** section, in the **Available fields** list box, select **Product.Product Name** and add it to the **On change of** list box.
   c) In the **Available fields** list box, select **Orders_Detail.Quantity** and add it to the **Show value(s)** list box.

3. Provide a title for the chart.
   a) On the **Text** tab, in the **Titles** section, uncheck the **Auto-Text** check box corresponding to the **Title** text box.
   b) In the **Title** text box, select the existing text and type *Helmet Types Sold*
   c) Select **OK** to create the chart.
   d) Preview the report.
   e) Verify that the chart displays the subtitle **For Alley Cat Cycles** and also shows the percentage of helmet types sold by that particular customer.
   a) Save the report as *My Total Helmet Sales* and close it.

---

# TOPIC F

## Format a Chart

You created charts for grouped data. You may now want to apply formatting to charts.

While creating a report, you don't often get the results you want the first time. You may want to format the report based on specific requirements. Similarly, you may not like the initial results of a chart being created and want to format it quickly and easily.

### The Chart Options Dialog Box

The **Chart Options** dialog box contains formatting tabs you can use to format a chart and also change its title and legends.

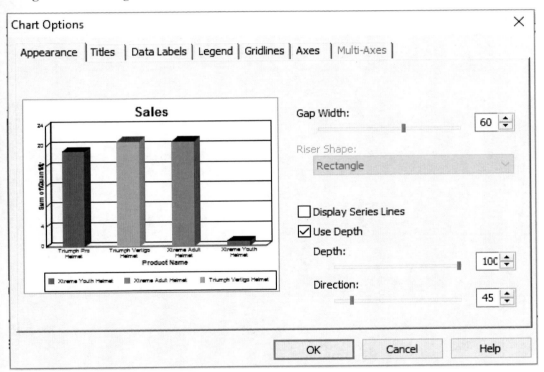

*Figure 7–3: Tabs in the Chart Options dialog box.*

The following table provides a description of each of the tabs available in this dialog box.

| Tab | Contains Options For |
| --- | --- |
| **Appearance** | Formatting display aspects of pie pieces, bars, lines, and other charts. |
| **Titles** | Changing the title, subtitle, footnote, group title, and data title. |
| **Data labels** | Specifying settings for data labels. |
| **Legend** | Specifying settings for legends. |
| **Gridlines** | Displaying gridlines on group and data axes. |
| **Axes** | Specifying settings for group and data axes. |
| **Multi-Axes** | Specifying where groups appear on what axis in a split bar chart. |

## Chart Formatting Options

In addition to the **Chart Options** dialog box, you can use the **Format Axis Label, Format Series Riser, Format Legend Entry, Format Data Label, Format Zero Line, Format Series Marker,** and **Format Chart Frame** dialog boxes to format charts.

 **Access the Checklist tile on your CHOICE Course screen for reference information and job aids on How to Format a Chart.**

# ACTIVITY 7-6
## Formatting a Chart

### Data Files

C:\095203Data\xtreme_B.mdb

C:\095203Data\Adding Charts to Reports\My Glove Helmet Sales.rpt

### Before You Begin

The Crystal Reports application is open.

### Scenario

You have a chart that shows one set of data for helmet sales. You are planning to add glove sales data to the same chart.

---

1. Change the type and layout of the chart and then specify the chart data.
   a) Open the **My Glove Helmet Sales.rpt** file.
   b) In the **Design** view, right-click the chart and select **Chart Expert**.
   c) In the **Chart Expert** dialog box, on the **Type** tab, check the **Use depth effect** check box.
   d) On the **Data** tab, in the **Layout** section, select **Advanced**.
   e) In the **Available Fields** list box, add the **Customer.Country** field to the **On change of** list box.
   f) Add the **Gloves** summary field to the **Show value(s)** list box.
   g) Add the **Helmets** summary field to the **Show value(s)** list box.

2. Change the chart titles and the location of legends.
   a) Select the **Options** tab.
   b) On the **Options** tab, in the **Data points** section, verify that the **Show label** check box is unchecked.
   c) In the **Legend** section, from the **Placement** drop-down list, select **Bottom**.
   d) On the **Text** tab, in the **Titles** section, in the **Title** text box, change the text to *Helmets and Gloves Sold Per Country*
   e) In the **Data title** text box, delete the text, and then select **OK**.

3. Change the legend headings.
   a) Preview the report, and with the chart selected, select the **Sum of @Helmets** label so that a selection border appears around it.
   b) Right-click the label and choose **Edit Axis Label**.
   c) In the **Label Aliasing** dialog box, in the **Displayed Label** text box, type *Helmets* and select **OK**.
   d) Select the **Sum of @Gloves** label.
   e) Right-click the label and select **Edit Axis Label**.
   f) In the **Label Aliasing** dialog box, in the **Displayed Label** text box, type *Gloves* and select **OK**.

4. Move the data labels to the base of the chart.
   a) Right-click the chart and select **Chart Options**.
   b) In the **Chart Options** dialog box, select the **Data Labels** tab, and from the **Labels Location** drop-down list, select **Base of Chart**.
   c) Verify that in the **Label Format** drop-down list, **Value** is selected, and then select **OK**.

5. Format the data labels.
   a) In the chart, select the **Austria** axis label, then right-click and select **Format Axis Label**.

b) In the **Format Axis Labels** dialog box, on the **Font** tab, select the **Bold** button.

c) From the **Size** drop-down list, select **10**, and then select **OK**.

d) Select the dark-blue data series riser, then right-click and select **Format Series Riser**.

e) In the **Format Series Riser** dialog box, select the **Foreground Color** drop-down arrow, and on the color palette, select the **(125, 181, 255)** color in the seventh row, tenth column, and then select **OK**.

f) Verify that in the 3D chart, the color of the series riser for glove sales has changed to a light blue.

g) Save and close the report.

# TOPIC G

# Create a Chart Template

You applied formatting to a chart. You may now want to create more charts with the same formatting.

You formatted and distributed charts to your client. You received a positive comment on your work. They want you to create more charts that look just like the ones you created earlier. You could probably duplicate the appearance of the charts, but it would be time-consuming and you may accidentally leave out some of the formatting. By creating a chart template, you will be able to apply the same formatting to numerous charts as required, saving time and effort.

## Chart Templates

A *chart template* is a saved set of chart formatting options you can apply to an existing chart using the **Choose a Chart type** dialog box. You can save a set of chart settings as a user-defined chart template.

 **Note:** You must apply templates carefully, because they will override the summary field in the chart and use the first summary field in the report.

 **Access the Checklist tile on your CHOICE Course screen for reference information and job aids on How to Create a Chart Template.**

# ACTIVITY 7-7
## Creating a Chart Template

### Data Files

C:\095203Data\xtreme_B.mdb

C:\095203Data\Adding Charts to Reports\Regional Sales.rpt

### Before You Begin

The Crystal Reports application is open.

### Scenario

You have spent a considerable amount of time with a coworker determining the format options for a chart. You want to incorporate the same formatting into all future financial reports.

1. Save the formatting from the **Last Year's Sales by Country** chart as a template.
   a) Open the **Regional Sales.rpt** file.
   b) In the **Design** view, right-click the **Last Year's Sales by Country** chart and select **Save as Template**.
   c) In the **Save As** dialog box, in the **File name** text box, select the existing text, type *Financial Charts* and then select **Save**.

2. Apply the created template.
   a) In the **Design** view, in the **GF1** section, right-click the chart and select **Load Template**.
   b) In the **Choose a Chart type** dialog box, on the **Custom** tab, in the **Categories** list box, select **User Defined**.
   c) Verify that the **Financial Charts** template is selected in the right pane, and then select **OK**.
   d) Preview the report and scroll down.
   e) Verify that the formatting of the **Last Year's Sales by Country** chart is applied to the **Top-Three Regions** chart.
   f) Save the report as *My Regional Sales* and close it.

# Summary

In this lesson, you added charts to a report and modified them. Adding charts to your reports enables you to present data in a report graphically.

**What are the advantages of using charts?**

**What types of reports in your environment would benefit from including charts in them?**

 **Note:** Check your CHOICE Course screen for opportunities to interact with your classmates, peers, and the larger CHOICE online community about the topics covered in this course or other topics you are interested in. From the Course screen you can also access available resources for a more continuous learning experience.

# 8 | Enhancing Report Functionality

**Lesson Time: 1 hour, 5 minutes**

## Lesson Objectives

In this lesson, you will:

- Organize data based on a hierarchy.

- Create a dynamic image.

- Create a report alert.

- Create a geographic map.

## Lesson Introduction

You created charts to present report data. You now want to enhance the report by using the features available in SAP® Crystal Reports® 2016.

You created a report that many users will access frequently, and each user may have a specific need. However, reading through the entire report to locate the required data may be a time-consuming and tiring experience. Enhancing report functionality will allow you to add features that help enrich the users' report-viewing experience and also help them understand the report data better.

# TOPIC A

# Organize Data Based on a Hierarchy

You created charts for report data. However, the reports may still contain a large volume of data and may not be organized.

You have an employee report that lists employee names and titles, but doesn't indicate which employee reports to which supervisor. By grouping data hierarchically, you can view how data items relate to one another.

## Organize Data Using a Hierarchy

You can group report data to show hierarchical relationships.

You need to follow a set of guidelines while organizing data using a hierarchy.

- A hierarchical relationship must be inherent in the data that you use for the report.
- The parent and child fields must be of the same data type for the program to recognize a relationship between them.
- The data in the parent field must be a subset of the data in the child field.
- For the top level of a hierarchy to appear in a report, its value must appear in the child data, and the parent data in that row must be empty.

 **Note:** There can't be any circular logic; that is, **A** cannot be related to **B**, while **B** is related to **C**, and **C** is related back to **A**.

### Data Organized Using a Hierarchy Example

Your organization is planning to conduct an annual meeting. As part of the planning, you decide to divide the event team into groups. A few employees have volunteered to act as team leaders for the groups. You have a list of the volunteers with details on responsibilities allocated to each of them.

You have also organized the data in a report to show the hierarchical relationship between the volunteers and the members of the group. You want each team leader's name, which is the parent field, to be of the same data type as the team members who constitute the child field. The team leaders' names should be a subset of the team members' names. For the manager's name to appear at the top level of the hierarchy, the value for his name must be in the child data. Because he is at the top level of the hierarchy, he will not have parent data.

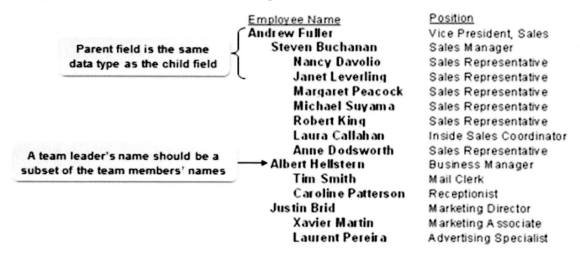

*Figure 8-1: Example of data organized using a hierarchy.*

## The HierarchyLevel Function

The **HierarchyLevel** function returns a number that indicates the hierarchy level of the current group member. It requires the **GroupingLevel** function, which determines the level of an existing group as an argument. The following example returns the level number of each member in your hierarchy, assuming that your report is grouped hierarchically based on the **Employee ID** field:

```
HierarchyLevel (GroupingLevel ({Employee.Employee ID}))
```

## Report Characteristics

In addition to the visual representation of the hierarchy inherent in the data, a report that's grouped hierarchically has several other characteristics. When you drill down into a group in the hierarchy, the ensuing drill-down view also shows the records that are lower in the hierarchy. The report contains hierarchical group footers that include the records that are lower in the hierarchy of each group. You can also summarize data across the hierarchies.

## The Hierarchical Group Options Dialog Box

You can use the **Hierarchical Group Options** dialog box to organize data hierarchically. You can access this dialog box from the **Report** menu. In this dialog box, you can specify the group to be organized and the field to be used for organizing the data.

## Indenting the Group Name Object

When you indent data using the **Group Indent** text box in the **Hierarchical Group Options** dialog box, all the fields get indented. You can use the **Object Size and Position** dialog box to indent only the group name object and display all other fields in their original location. You can also create a conditional formula that will indent group name fields in all hierarchical levels. The measurement scale used in the formula is *twips*. The equivalent of 1 inch is 1,440 twips.

 **Access the Checklist tile on your CHOICE Course screen for reference information and job aids on How to Organize Data Based on a Hierarchy.**

# ACTIVITY 8–1
## Organizing Data Based on a Hierarchy

### Before You Begin
- Crystal Reports is open.
- Create a blank report and connect to the **xtreme_B.mdb** database in the **C:\095203Data** folder.
- Add the **Employee** table.

### Scenario
As the manager of human resources, you are planning to create a list of all employees in your organization. You also want to document information about the reporting managers, their positions, and the incremental salaries.

---

1. Group the new report by employee ID and customize the group by using the employee's last name.
   a) In the **Field Explorer**, expand **Database Fields**, and then expand **Employee**.
   b) From the **Employee** table, drag the **Position** field to the 2-inch mark in the **Details** section.
   c) From the **Employee** table, drag the **Salary** field to the 4-inch mark in the **Details** section.
   d) On the **Insert** toolbar, select the **Insert Group** button.
   e) In the **Insert Group** dialog box, from the first drop-down list, select **Employee ID**.
   f) In the second drop-down list, verify that **in ascending order** is selected.

2. Create a conditional formula that will output the first name and the last name as one field.
   a) On the **Options** tab, check the **Customize Group Name Field** check box.
   b) Select the **Use a Formula as Group Name** option, and then select the **Conditional Formula** button.
   c) In the **Definition** area, type the following code that will output the first and last names as one field:

      `{Employee.First Name} + " " + {Employee.Last Name}`
   d) Check the formula for errors, and then select **Save and close**.
   e) In the **Insert Group** dialog box, select **OK**.

3. Move the fields in the **Details** section up to the **GH1** section.
   a) In the blue area of the **Details** section, right-click and select the **Select All Section Objects** option.
   b) Move the **Position** and **Salary** fields to the 2- and 4-inch marks of the **GH1** section, respectively.

4. Group the data hierarchically by supervisor ID.
   a) Select **Report→Hierarchical Grouping Options**.
   b) In the **Hierarchical Group Options** dialog box, check the **Sort Data Hierarchically** check box.
   c) From the **Parent ID Field** drop-down list, select **Supervisor ID**.
   d) In the **Group Indent** box, verify that zero is displayed, and then select **OK**.
   e) In the **GH1** section, right-click the **Group #1 Employee ID** field and select **Size and Position**.
   f) In the **Object Size and Position** dialog box, select the first **Conditional Formula** button.
   g) In the **Definition** area, type the following code to group hierarchically by supervisor ID:

      `(HierarchyLevel (GroupingLevel ({Employee.Employee ID}))-1) * 1440/4`

       **Note:** The formula indents only the **Group #1 Employee ID** object, depending on its hierarchy position. The lower the hierarchy, the more the object is indented.
   h) Check the formula for errors, and then select **Save and close**.
   i) In the **Object Size and Position** dialog box, select **OK**.

5. Suppress the unnecessary sections.

    a) On the **Experts** toolbar, select the **Section Expert** button.

    b) In the **Section Expert** dialog box, in the **Sections** section, select **Details**, and then check the **Suppress (No Drill-Down)** check box.

    c) Suppress the **Group Footer #1: Employee.Employee ID - A**, **Page Footer**, and **Report Footer** sections.

    d) In the **Section Expert** dialog box, select **OK**.

6. Insert a text object and preview the report.

    a) On the **Insert** toolbar, select the **Insert Text Object** button.

    b) In the left margin of the **PH** section, click and drag the pointer to create a box.

    c) In the text box, type *Employee Name*

    d) Click away from the text object to deselect it.

    e) Select the **Employee Name** text object, and on the **Standard** toolbar, select the **Underline** button.

    f) Preview the report.

    g) Save the report as *My Employee Hierarchy* in the C:\095203Data\Enhancing Report Functionality folder and close the report.

# TOPIC B

# Create a Dynamic Image

You organized data based on a hierarchy. Now you want to add images to a report and be able to change them as needed without accessing the report.

Suppose you have used an image in several reports and there may be situations when you want to update the image. By creating dynamic images, you will be able to update images in your report as requirements change. Also, as the report creator, you can update images externally without accessing the report.

## OLE Objects

An *Object Linking and Embedding (OLE) object* is a picture or metafile stored on a shared network and accessed by a file path or URL. The file path or URL is typically stored as a string field in a database. The pictures or metafiles on the network change frequently. Static OLE and dynamic OLE are the two types of OLE objects.

 **Note:** When a dynamic OLE object is not found in the specified location, the latest version of the OLE object is displayed.

 **Note:** The dynamic OLE object feature is activated when you refresh your report data; therefore, you may not notice a change in the static OLE object until you select the **Refresh** button in Crystal Reports.

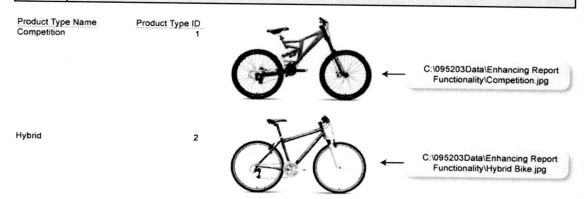

*Figure 8-2: OLE objects.*

 Access the Checklist tile on your **CHOICE Course** screen for reference information and job aids on **How to Create a Dynamic Image.**

# ACTIVITY 8–2
## Creating a Dynamic Image

### Data Files

C:\095203Data\xtreme_B.mdb

C:\095203Data\Enhancing Report Functionality\Products List.rpt

C:\095203Data\Enhancing Report Functionality\Product List.xls

C:\095203Data\Enhancing Report Functionality\Openfile.jpg

C:\095203Data\Enhancing Report Functionality\Helmet.jpg

C:\095203Data\Enhancing Report Functionality\Adult Helmet.jpg

### Before You Begin

Crystal Reports is open.

### Scenario

As the reporting specialist for the company, you want to incorporate graphics into reports to display information in a different manner. As new products emerge, images of products your company sells tend to change from season to season. You want to incorporate these dynamic images into your reports to account for and display these cyclical changes.

1. Insert a picture in the **Details** section.
   a) Open the **Products List.rpt** file.
   b) In the **Design** view, on the **Insert** toolbar, select the **Insert Picture** button.
   c) If necessary, in the **Open** dialog box, navigate to the **C:\095203Data\Enhancing Report Functionality** folder.
   d) Select the **Openfile.jpg** file, and then select **Open**.
   e) In the **Details** section, click at the 4.5-inch mark to place the picture.

2. Create a link for the dynamic images.
   a) Right-click the picture and select **Format Graphic**.
   b) In the **Format Editor** dialog box, select the **Picture** tab, and in the **Graphic** section, select the **Conditional Formula** button.
   c) In the **Formula Workshop - Format Formula Editor - Graphic Location** dialog box, in the **Field Tree**, expand **C:\095203Data\Enhancing Report Functionality\Product List.xls(Access/Excel (DAO))**, expand **Sheet1_**, and then double-click **Image Location**.
   d) Check the formula for errors, and then select **Save and close**.
   e) In the **Format Editor** dialog box, select **OK**.
   f) Preview the report and view all the images.
   g) Verify that the picture of the helmet is upside down.

    **Note:** You will be replacing this image with the correct one, making sure the image name continues to map to the Excel file.

   h) Save the report as *My Products List*
   i) In the **Unable To Save Data With Report** message box, select **Yes**.
   j) Close the report.

3. Delete the incorrect image and update the correct image name to match the Excel file.

    a) Navigate to the **C:\095203Data\Enhancing Report Functionality** folder and delete the **Adult Helmet.jpg** file.

    b) Rename the current **Helmet.jpg** file to *Adult Helmet.jpg* to match the name in the Excel file.

4. Open the **My Products List** file and refresh the data.

    a) Open the **My Products List** file in Crystal Reports.

    b) On the **Navigation** toolbar, select the **Refresh** button.

    c) In the **Refresh Report Data** message box, select **OK**.

    d) Verify that the helmet image is displayed correctly.

    e) Save the report.

    f) In the **Unable To Save Data With Report** message box, select **Yes**.

    g) Close the report.

 **Note:** To explore how to customize reports, access the Spotlight on **Using Images Creatively** presentation from the **Spotlight** tile on the CHOICE course screen.

# TOPIC C

# Create a Report Alert

You created dynamic images in a report that can be updated without accessing the file. You may now want to convey information to users when a particular condition is met by the data in the report.

You have created a report that lists the net profit of various companies for this quarter. You want to convey information to users when the company gains a profit above a certain value. By creating a report alert, you will be able to convey information to users effectively.

## Report Alerts

A *report alert* is a custom message that either contains information about report data or conveys the action the user must take. Report alerts are created from formulas that evaluate conditions you specify. If a condition is true, an alert is triggered and its message is displayed. After a report alert is triggered, the formula will not check for the condition again unless the report is refreshed again.

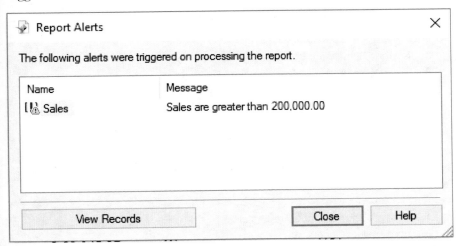

*Figure 8–3: Report alerts.*

## Alert Formulas in Crystal Reports

Alert formulas can be based on recurring records or on summary fields, but can't be based on print-time fields, such as running totals or print-time formulas. In addition, alert formulas can't have shared variables.

 **Access the Checklist tile on your CHOICE Course screen for reference information and job aids on How to Create a Report Alert.**

# ACTIVITY 8–3
## Creating a Report Alert

### Data Files

C:\095203Data\xtreme_B.mdb

C:\095203Data\Enhancing Report Functionality\Amount of International Sales.rpt

### Before You Begin

The Crystal Reports application is open.

### Scenario

As the manager of the sales department, you want your team to be up-to-date on the current sales numbers. You want a report that will point out important information regarding fluctuating sales limits above a given range.

1. Insert a report alert to check whether the previous year's sales are greater than the target.
   a) Select **Open File** to display the **Open** dialog box.
   b) Navigate to the **C:\095203Data\Enhancing Report Functionality** folder.
   c) Select the **Amount of International Sales.rpt** file, and then select **Open**.
   d) Select **Report→Alerts→Create or Modify Alerts**.
   e) In the **Create Alerts** dialog box, select **New**.
   f) In the **Create Alert** dialog box, in the **Name** text box, type *Sales*
   g) To the right of the **Message** text box, select the **Conditional Formula** button.
   h) In the **Formula Workshop - Alert Message Formula Editor** window, in the **Definition** area, enter the following conditional formula code that will display a message for the alert:

      ```
      "Sales are greater than " + ToText ({?Amount of Sales})
      ```
   i) Check the formula for errors, and then select **Save and close**.
   j) In the **Create Alert** dialog box, select **Condition**.
   k) In the **Formula Workshop - Alert Condition Formula Editor** window, type the following conditional formula code that will create the alert:

      ```
      {Customer.Last Year's Sales} > {?Amount of Sales}
      ```
   l) Check the formula for errors, and then select **Save and close**.
   m) In the **Create Alert** dialog box, verify that the **Enabled** check box is checked, and then select **OK**.
   n) In the **Create Alerts** dialog box, select **Close**.

2. View the alert for the report.
   a) On the **Navigation** toolbar, select the **Refresh** button.
   b) In the **Refresh Report Data** dialog box, select the **Prompt for new parameter values** option, and then select **OK**.
   c) In the **Enter Values** dialog box, from the **Enter Amount of Sales** drop-down list, select **200,000**, and then select **OK**.
   d) In the **Report Alerts** dialog box, view the message that is displayed, select **Sales**, and then select **View Records**.
   e) Verify that the report displays sales greater than or equal to $200,000.
   f) Save the report as *My Amount of International Sales* and close it.

# TOPIC D

# Create a Geographic Map

You created alerts for your report. Maps are another method of enhancing a report. If you want to represent data based on geography, there's no better option than using maps.

The products manufactured by your company are used all over the world. You want to present the sales data as a map, highlighting or color-coding the different regions with the highest sales. By creating a geographic map, you will be able to interpret large amounts of data quickly and easily.

## The Map Expert Dialog Box

You can use the **Map Expert** dialog box to create a geographic map and specify settings for the map.

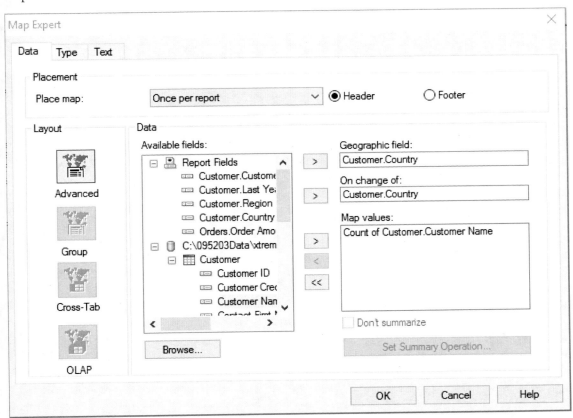

*Figure 8-4: The Data tab selected in the Map Expert dialog box.*

The following table lists the tabs and their function.

| Tab | Allows You To |
| --- | --- |
| **Data** | Specify the type of layout to be used. |
| **Type** | Specify the type of map to be used. You should select the type based on the data to be analyzed. |
| **Text** | Specify the title for the map and for the legends. |

**Note:** To explore how to customize reports, access the Spotlight on **Using Map Features in Reports** presentation from the **Spotlight** tile on the CHOICE course screen.

 **Access the Checklist tile on your CHOICE Course screen for reference information and job aids on How to Create a Geographic Map.**

# ACTIVITY 8–4
## Creating a Geographic Map

### Data File
C:\095203Data\xtreme_B.mdb

### Before You Begin
The Crystal Reports application is open.

### Scenario
Xtreme Bicycle sells products internationally, and you have decided to create a geographic map that shows customer density by country. You're planning to use six different colors showing the number of customers in the countries, with white as the lowest and red as the highest. The darker the color, the more customers in that country.

1. Create a report to view the distribution of customers across the world.
   a) Select **File→New→Blank Report**.
   b) In the **Database Expert** dialog box, on the **Data** tab, in the **Available Data Sources** list box, expand **C:\095203Data\xtreme_B.mdb**.
   c) Expand **Tables**, and then add the **Customer** table to the **Selected Tables** list box.
   d) Select **OK**.

2. Insert a map based on the regional distribution of customers.
   a) Select **Insert→Map**.
   b) In the **Map Expert** dialog box, on the **Data** tab, in the **Available fields** list box, scroll down and select **Country**, and add it to the **Geographic field** text box.
   c) Verify that the **Customer.Country** field is automatically added to the **On change of** text box.
   d) Scroll up and add the **Customer Name** field to the **Map values** list box.
   e) Verify that the default summary value changes to **Count** because **Customer Name** is a text field.

3. Set different map options.
   a) Select the **Type** tab.
   b) Verify that the **Ranged** map type is selected.
   c) In the **Options** section, in the **Number of intervals** text box, double-click and type *7*
   d) Select the **Color of highest interval** drop-down arrow, and on the color palette, select **Red**.
   e) Select the **Color of lowest interval** drop-down arrow, and on the color palette, select **White**.

4. Define legend titles for the report.
   a) Select the **Text** tab.
   b) In the **Legend** section, verify that the **Full legend** option is selected.
   c) In the **Legend title** section, select the **Specify** option.
   d) In the **Title** text box, type *Customer Locations* and then press **Tab**.
   e) In the **Subtitle** text box, type *By Country* and then select **OK**.
   f) In the **RH** section, drag the middle-right sizing handle of the map to the 6.5-inch mark.

5. Preview and save the report.
   a) Preview the report and select the map.

    b) Position the mouse pointer over **Canada** and verify that the tooltip displays the number of customers in that country.

    c) Save the report as *My Customer Locations* and close it.

>  **Note:** To explore how to customize reports, access the Spotlight on **The Crystal Reports Community** presentation from the **Spotlight** tile on the CHOICE course screen.

# Summary

In this lesson, you enhanced report functionality. Enhancing report functionality will help users understand the report data better.

**What types of data will you group hierarchically in your report?**


**For which types of data will you create report alerts? Why?**

 **Note:** To explore how to customize reports, access the Spotlight on **Expanding Crystal Reports' Capabilities** presentation from the **Spotlight** tile on the CHOICE course screen.

 **Note:** Check your CHOICE Course screen for opportunities to interact with your classmates, peers, and the larger CHOICE online community about the topics covered in this course or other topics you are interested in. From the Course screen you can also access available resources for a more continuous learning experience.

# Course Follow-Up

Congratulations! You have completed the *SAP® Crystal Reports® 2016: Part 2* course. In this course, you created complex reports. By taking time to learn how to use some of the tools in Crystal Reports, you won't be slowed down by large or unfamiliar databases. By creating subreports, cross-tabs, and running totals, you will turn raw data into meaningful, customized reports that will help your business run more smoothly.

## What's Next?

You are encouraged to explore Crystal Reports further by actively participating in any of the social media forums set up by your instructor or training administrator through the **Social Media** tile on the CHOICE Course screen.

# Managing Reports

## The BusinessObjects Enterprise

BusinessObjects Enterprise provides an effective way to deliver your reports over the web or to integrate them into custom web applications. The Report Application Server (RAS) supplies a rich set of server-based reporting services focused on report processing, application integration, and runtime report modification.

You can extend your application even further using the advanced services available in other editions of BusinessObjects Enterprise, including the following:

- **Security:** Granular group, user, and data-level security help you protect sensitive reports and deliver a more personalized end-user experience.
- **Scheduling:** A flexible time- and event-based scheduling system allows you to process large reports during off hours and avoid unnecessary database hits.
- **Versioning:** Works closely with scheduling to store "instances" of a report. Versioning not only reduces the number of database hits required to serve users, but also allows you to keep an archive of report instances for historical reference.
- **Clustering:** Incorporates proven clustering and load-balancing technology.
- **Scalability:** BusinessObjects Enterprise is built on a distributed, multi-server architecture, allowing you to scale up on a single machine (by adding processors) or scale out over multiple machines to handle heavier user loads.
- **Management:** Incorporates extensive administration and management controls that allow you to organize content, set up complex schedules and security, and tune the system for optimal performance.
- **External (Third-Party) Authentication:** Allows you to leverage your existing security system to manage users and groups. You can delegate all authentication to a third-party NT or Lightweight Directory Access Protocol (LDAP) system.

## BusinessObjects Enterprise Repository

The BusinessObjects Enterprise Repository is the central location for storing and managing report objects. It's a database hosted by the Central Management Server of BusinessObjects Enterprise that stores object types, including text objects, bitmaps, custom functions, and custom SQL commands. The objects contained in the repository are then accessible to users and report developers for use in their reports.

You can modify a particular object in the shared repository and, when reports containing that object are opened for use, the object is updated in the report.

The BusinessObjects Enterprise Repository is contained in the BusinessObjects Enterprise.

You can use the **Repository Explorer** pane to add reports, text objects, and bitmaps to the repository. You can add custom functions to the repository through the **Formula Workshop** window. You can also add subfolders and subcategories to the repository to help organize the contents more efficiently.

### The Workbench

You can use the **Workbench** pane to organize reports. In this pane, you can create project folders that contain one or more reports. You can use the options on the toolbar to add, remove, or rename folders, reports, and object packages. You can also reorganize the files in a folder or folders by dragging and dropping them where you want them to appear.

You can create project folders containing one or more report files. You can add an object package only when the Enterprise connectivity exists. You can save the project folders to the BusinessObjects Enterprise Repository.

### Working with Local Reports

Local reports refer to those reports that have been stored on the local system. Crystal Reports saves a report on the local system only when the connection to the repository is broken. When the connection is reestablished, the changes to the local copy are uploaded to the file in the repository automatically. When the Enterprise connectivity exists, local reports are not saved. The reports are saved directly to the repository.

# B | Processing Data on the Server

## Optimizing Record Selection

Crystal Reports 2016 contains some drivers for SQL data sources that enable you to optimize records while retrieving data from the server. By optimizing record selection, you can reduce the number of records by filtering the data during the processing stage. This process happens in the following two stages:

1. In the first stage of record selection, the SQL query is processed by the data server and a set of records based on the query is generated and sent to Crystal Reports.
2. During the second stage, Crystal Reports locally evaluates the record selection formula for the set of records retrieved from the database server.

You need to specify record selection formulas that enable the server to process data in the first stage itself. By doing this, you can reduce the number of records being retrieved from the server to the local machine. This process is called *optimizing record selection*. The record selections you can optimize are SQL queries that contain OR and AND clauses, selections that contain indexed and non-indexed fields, and SQL expression fields that execute formula calculations for optimizing record selection.

 **Note:** You can optimize record selection faster using indexed fields.

## Performing Grouping on a Server

The **Performing Grouping on a Server** option in the **Report Options** and **Options** dialog boxes enables you to accomplish grouping of data on the server, also known as server-side processing. By enabling this option, you can ensure that a majority of the report data is processed on the server side and only relevant details are passed on to the client system. Server-side processing has the following benefits:

- The time taken to connect to the server is reduced.
- Because a majority of data is processed on the server, the amount of memory used on the client system is minimal.
- Time taken for the data to be transferred from the server to the client is less.

However, you can enable server-side processing only in reports that are based on SQL data sources.

# C | Detecting and Fixing Problems

## Finding Resources to Fix Issues

When you find issues with Crystal Reports, you can access Crystal Reports built-in help or visit the links provided in the **Key Resources** tab on the **SAP Crystal Reports - Start Page**.

# Mastery Builders

Mastery Builders are provided for certain lessons as additional learning resources for this course. Mastery Builders are developed for selected lessons within a course in cases when they seem most instructionally useful as well as technically feasible. In general, Mastery Builders are supplemental, optional unguided practice and may or may not be performed as part of the classroom activities. Your instructor will consider setup requirements, classroom timing, and instructional needs to determine which Mastery Builders are appropriate for you to perform, and at what point during the class. If you do not perform the Mastery Builders in class, your instructor can tell you if you can perform them independently as self-study, and if there are any special setup requirements.

# Mastery Builder 1–1
## Creating a Running Total Field

### Activity Time: 10 minutes

### Data File
C:\095203Data\Creating Running Totals\ShippingInfo.rpt

### Before You Begin
The Crystal Reports application is open.

### Scenario
You work for a company that sells bicycles and related equipment. As the manager of the shipping department, you maintain a report called **ShippingInfo.rpt** to track orders. You now want to find out the number of orders that were shipped by UPS and FedEx as of May 1, 2014.

 **Note:** Page header labels have already been placed in the report for running totals. Remove extra field labels when not needed.

1. Open the **ShippingInfo.rpt** file.

2. Create a running total called *UPS* that summarizes the **Ship Via** field.
   - Evaluation formula: `{Orders.Ship Via}= "UPS"`
   - Function: `Count`

3. Create a running total for all **FedEx** shipments and name it *FedEx*
   - Evaluation formula: `{Orders.Ship Via}= "FedEx"`
   - Function: `Count`

4. Add the **FedEx** and **UPS** running total fields to the report, under their respective headings.

5. Preview the report and verify that there are running totals for UPS and FedEx shipments.

6. Save the report as *My ShippingInfo* and close it.

# Mastery Builder 2–1
## Creating a Cross–Tab Report

**Activity Time: 10 minutes**

### Data File
C:\095203Data\xtreme_B.mdb

### Before You Begin
The Crystal Reports application is open.

### Scenario
You work for a company that sells bicycles and related spare parts. You want to find out the total count of orders by year and shipment type, in a grid format. Your users are particularly interested in the FedEx and UPS totals, so you decide to show those two shipment carriers as the first item in your grid.

---

1. Create a blank report using the **Orders** table in the **xtreme_B.mdb** file.

2. In the **Report Header (RH)** section, create a cross-tab and insert a row heading in the **Ship Date** field, grouped by year.

3. Insert a column heading using the **Ship Via** field.

4. Change the grouping options for the **Ship Via** field to present **FedEx** and **UPS** values first and then all the others in their own groups.

5. Insert a summary field that counts the **Order ID**.

6. Preview the report.

7. Decrease the decimal places of the counts of orders.

8. Change the page orientation so the report prints on one page.

9. Save the report as *My Shipping* and close it.

---

# Mastery Builder 3–1
## Correlating Data Using a Subreport

**Activity Time: 25 minutes**

### Data Files

C:\095203Data\Adding Subreports\Orders.rpt

C:\095203Data\Adding Subreports\Credits.rpt

### Before You Begin

The Crystal Reports application is open.

### Scenario

You work for a company that sells bicycles and related equipment. You have a report, **Orders.rpt**, that displays total customer orders, and another report, **Credits.rpt**, that displays total customer credits. You desire to view both the customer orders information and the customer credits information in a single report. You want the customer credits information to appear on-demand because you need it only when you prepare monthly or quarterly reports. Because the sales are continuing to expand, you always want the updated information in your report.

---

1. Open the **Orders.rpt** file.

2. Insert the **Credits.rpt** file as an on-demand subreport, link it to the primary report by the **Customer ID** field, and place it in the group header under the **Credits** page header.

3. Modify the subreport by deleting the **Report Footer b (RFb)** section.

4. Update both the **On-Demand Subreport Caption** and the **Subreport Preview Tab Caption** to *Credit*

5. Preview the on-demand subreport.

   If you click to preview several customers' credits, you will have multiple tabs open which all say **Credits**. This is confusing, so you want to change each **Subreport Preview Tab Caption**.

6. Update the **Subreport Preview Tab Caption** to say *Credits:* and the customer's name.

7. Preview the on-demand subreport and verify that the tab captions are correct.

   Although you like the new tab captions, you don't like having to click each **Credit** link to see which customer has a credit.

8. Replace the on-demand subreport with a regular credit subreport and suppress any reports for customers who do not have credits.

9. Preview the report and verify that credits are listed for all customers who have credits and are blank for those customers without credits.

10. Edit the subreport to remove the borders, remove the **Credit** label in each row, and remove the header and footer.

11. Preview the report and verify that the borders are removed and only the credit dollar amount is listed in those rows where customers have a credit.

12. Save the report as *My Subreport* and close it.

# Mastery Builder 4-1
## Creating a Drill-Down

**Activity Time:** 10 minutes

### Data File

C:\095203Data\Creating Drill-Downs\Position Salaries.rpt

### Before You Begin

The Crystal Reports application is open.

### Scenario

You work for an engineering firm and are creating a report to display the total salary expenses for each department. Although you don't need to display the salaries for each employee in each department in the primary report, you want that data to be accessible from within the report.

---

1. Open the **Position Salaries.rpt** file.

2. Group the employees by their position and also insert a summary to calculate the salary of all employees in each group.

3. Move the summary field to the 3-inch mark in the **Group Header #1: Employee.Position - A** section.

4. Hide the **Details** section so that its contents are visible only for a drill-down.

5. In the **Details** section, add the **First Name**, **Last Name**, and **Salary** fields.

6. Format the salaries to appear as currency with the style **$(1,123.00)**.

7. Insert a group header section below the **Group Header #1 Employee.Position - A** section and move the **First Name**, **Last Name**, and **Salary** field labels from the **Page Header (PH)** section to the newly added section.

8. Suppress the **Group Header #1b: Employee.Position - A** section in the primary report.

9. At the 0-inch mark in the **Page Header (PH)** section, add a text object named *Position Salary Expenses*

10. Preview the drill-down data.

11. Save the report as *My Position Salaries* and close it.

---

# Mastery Builder 5-1
## Enhancing Report Processing Using SQL

**Activity Time: 10 minutes**

### Data File
C:\095203Data\xtreme_B.mdb

### Before You Begin
The Crystal Reports application is open.

### Scenario
You work for a company that distributes bicycles and equipment to shops around the world. You want to specify an SQL query to create a report that lists all customers alphabetically and includes the largest order amount from each customer. The data that you require is present in two different tables: **Customer** and **Orders**. Both of these tables contain a common field called **Customer ID**.

---

1. Create a new blank report using the **Add Command** option for the **xtreme_B.mdb** database file.

2. Write an SQL statement that will generate the desired report.

3. Move the generated fields onto the **Details** section of the report layout.

4. Preview the report and adjust the formatting as desired.

5. Save the report as *My Largest Orders.rpt* and close it.

---

# Mastery Builder 6–1
## Creating a Complex Formula

**Lesson Time: 10 minutes**

### Data File

C:\095203Data\Creating Complex Formula\Customer Payments.rpt

### Before You Begin

The Crystal Reports application is open.

### Scenario

You are the finance manager of your company. Some of your customers haven't paid for goods that have been delivered. You want to identify those customers.

---

1.  Open the **Customer Payments.rpt** file.

2.  Place the **Customer** parameter in the **Report Header (RH)** section and suppress it.

3.  In the **Select Expert -- Record** dialog box, on the **Customer.Customer Name** tab, enter the following formula for filtering records that need to be displayed based on the values entered in the parameter:

    ```
    numberVar n:=1;
    numberVar Position:=count({?Customer});
    stringVar Array CustName;
    while Position >= n do
    (
    Redim Preserve CustName[n];
    CustName[n] :={?Customer}[n];
    n:=n+1;
    );
    {Customer.Customer Name} in CustName
    ```

4.  Preview the report.

5.  In the **Enter Values** dialog box, select the country, and then select the customers for whom you want to view the records.

6.  Select **OK**.

7.  Save the report as *My Customer Payments* and close it.

---

# Mastery Builder 7–1
## Creating a Data Series Chart

**Activity Time: 10 minutes**

### Data File

C:\095203Data\Adding Charts to Reports\Qtr 1 Canada Sales.rpt

### Before You Begin

The Crystal Reports application is open.

### Scenario

You work for a company that sells bicycles and related equipment. You created a **Qtr 1 Canada Sales** report that shows the totals of the quarterly sales in Canada. The sales representatives tried innovative marketing with two of the customers, Crazy Wheels and Pedal Pusher Bikes, Inc., and have achieved success. You know that the other sales representatives will be more impressed if they can graphically see the increase in sales for these two customers.

1. Open the **Qtr 1 Canada Sales.rpt** file.

2. In the **Design** view, insert a new report header section in which to place your chart.

3. Insert a vertical bar chart into the report by performing the actions mentioned.
   a) Add the **Order Date** and **Customer Name** fields to the **On change of** list box.

    **Note:** Make sure the **Order Date** field appears above the **Customer Name** field so that the first graphing sort will be done by date.

   b) Add the **Order Amount** field to the **Show value(s)** list box.
   c) Change the settings to display **Data points** values with the format **1K**.
   d) Change the chart title to *First Quarter Sales* and data title to *Total Sales*
   e) Remove the group title text.

4. Make modifications to the chart using the **Chart Options** dialog box.
   a) Change the location of data labels to appear outside the data risers.
   b) Change the box style of legends to display legends in a reverse beveled box below the chart.
   c) Change the data riser shape to display them as beveled boxes.

5. Preview the chart.

6. Save the report as *My Qtr 1 Canada Sales* and close it.

# Mastery Builder 8–1
## Enhancing the Functionality of a Report

**Activity Time: 20 minutes**

### Data Files

C:\095203Data\Enhancing Report Functionality\Staff Salaries.rpt

C:\095203Data\Enhancing Report Functionality\Staff Salaries.xls

### Before You Begin

The Crystal Reports application is open.

### Scenario

You want to group employee data hierarchically and display an alert based on salary.

---

1. Open the **Staff Salaries.rpt** file.

2. Group the report by the **Emp #** field, and customize the group name to display the employee's first name and last name.

3. Remove the last name and first name columns from the report.

4. Place the **Position** and **Salary** fields at the 2- and 4-inch marks in the **Details** section.

5. Group the report data hierarchically by **Supervisor ID**.

6. Indent the **Group #1 Name** object using the **Object Size And Position** dialog box, and enter the following formula:

   ```
   (HierarchyLevel (GroupingLevel ({'DCT_Staff_txt_'.Emp #})) - 1) *
   1440/4
   ```

7. Place the **Salary Total** parameter in the **Report Footer (RF)** section.

8. Create an alert named *Salary* and enter the following formula for displaying a message:

   ```
   "Salaries are greater than " + totext({?Salary Total})
   ```

9. Enter the following formula for the condition to be checked when displaying the alert:

   ```
   {'DCT_Staff_txt_'.Salary}>{?Salary Total}
   ```

10. Move the **Position** and **Salary** fields to the **Group Header (GH)** section.

11. Preview the report.

12. In the **Enter Values** dialog box, enter a numeric value.

13. View the report alert, and then view the records that match the alert condition.

14. Suppress the **Details**, **Group Footer #1 (GF1)**, and **Report Footer (RF)** sections for a condensed display.

---

**15.** Save the file as *My Staff Salaries* and close it.

# Glossary

**alias**
An alternative name assigned to cross-tab row or column heading fields so that they can be used in formulas.

**array**
A data structure that contains a large amount of data of the same type.

**chart**
A graphical representation of data that makes it easier to analyze data.

**chart template**
A saved set of chart formatting options that can be used as the starting point for formatting a new chart.

**Count**
A function that enables you to count the values that appear in a report (with the exception of nulls) for a specified field.

**cross-tab**
A report presented in a column and row format. It is used to summarize and present data in a way that makes it easy to identify trends and compare data.

**cross-tab chart**
A chart type that displays the summary data from a cross-tab report.

**drill-down**
A feature that allows you to view detailed information about summarized data.

**join**
A method of linking two or more tables together so that data from all linked tables can be used within a single report.

**loop**
Programming logic that allows the user to execute a set of programming statements within it for a number of iterations.

**null**
A value indicating that no values exist within a database field for a given record.

**OLE object**
A picture or metafile that is accessed by using a file path or URL, which is typically stored as a string field in a database.

**on-demand subreport**
A subreport that can be accessed only by clicking the link for the subreport in the primary report.

**report alert**
A custom message that appears when certain data conditions are met in a report. Report alerts are created from formulas that evaluate conditions you specify.

**running total**
The summary value that is displayed for each record.

**server-side processing**
A report-processing technique that is carried out on the remote server containing

the database, rather than on the client computer.

### shared variable

A type of variable provided by Crystal Reports that enables you to pass data back and forth between primary reports and subreports or between subreports.

### SQL

(Structured Query Language) The standard query language that is used within other languages or applications to access and manipulate relational database data.

### SQL aggregate function

A function that produces a single summary value for a group of values in a specified field.

### SQL clauses

The components of an SQL statement that you use to indicate the task you want the database to perform.

### SQL expression field

A formula written in SQL that usually results in a calculated field that a report can use.

### SQL statement

A request that is written using SQL clauses and sent to a server containing an SQL database, directing the server to perform specific database tasks.

### subquery

A query that is nested inside an outer query.

### subreport

A report that can be created when a user wants to correlate data from two unrelated reports, or data that cannot be linked by any other method.

### summarized field

A field that represents a summary, such as a sum, count, or average of multiple values.

### top N chart

A chart type that allows you to narrow the data results displayed by specifying rank criteria.

### variable

A storage location in memory whose value can change as an application is running.

### variable scope

A variable designation that determines how long and where a variable keeps its value.

# Index

# R

Re-import When Opening option *38*
report alert *121*
report characteristics *115*
running total *2*

# S

server-side processing *58*
shared variable *43*
SQL
    aggregate functions *66*
    clauses *59*
    expression fields *78*
    overview *58*
    rules and conventions *60*
    statements *59, 74*
static array *87*
Structured Query Language, *See* SQL
subquery *74*
subreport
    on-demand *38*
    updating *38*
summarized field *18*

# T

top N chart *99*

# V

variables *10*
variable scope *44*

095203S rev 1.0
ISBN-13 978-1-4246-2682-3
ISBN-10 1-4246-2682-X

9 781424 626823        90000